AF476980
46143

On the North and West Route

from Chester to Newport

C.R.L.Coles

LONDON
IAN ALLAN LTD

Previous page:
4-6-2 locomotive No 6201 *Princess Elizabeth* **leaving Shrewsbury for Hereford with a 'Welsh Marches Express' on 18 April 1981.** *Peter J. C. Skelton*

Right:
A pictorial impression of Cefn Mawr viaduct, which spans the Vale of Llangollen, and over which preserved 4-6-0 No 5000 is heading an enthusiast's special on 23 October 1982. *Dr L. A. Nixon*

First published 1984

ISBN 0 7110 1408 6

Published by Ian Allan Ltd, Shepperton, Surrey; and printed by Ian Allan Printing Ltd at their works at Coombelands in Runnymede, England.

Contents

Preface

As its title implies, this is a pictorial coverage of a cross-country main line (and its one-time many branches) extending through four of the five counties in Great Britain which comprise the Welsh Marches — Gwent of which Monmouthshire is a part, Herefordshire, Shropshire and Cheshire. Montgomeryshire, now part of Powys, lies outside the route in question and accordingly has been excluded. Although from Shrewsbury southwards this is generally known as the North to West line, it would be equally correct to describe it the other way round and I have elected, for reasons which will speak for themselves, to follow the line northward from the Bristol Channel to Shrewsbury and Chester — a total distance of $137\frac{1}{2}$ route miles from Newport. In some respects this line can be said to be similar to any other if we confine ourselves to its main purpose and little else. But in other respects, this is far from the case.

Though they are an integral part of the railway and play a vital part in its contribution to the nation's needs, I am no less concerned about the trains themselves as I am with its many other principal characteristics. This equally applies to the country served by the railway. A study of the gradient profile shows this to be a predominantly hilly route with short steep inclines in both directions nearer the southern end and a long sustained up hill drag over nearly 40 miles from Hereford to Church Stretton followed by a somewhat steeper but shorter downhill gradient onward to Shrewsbury. Yet there are few outstanding civil engineering features over this stretch of line apart from bridges spanning the Rivers Usk, Wye, Severn and Dee. Excluding the Vale of Neath line (of which more later), there are no viaducts until beyond Shrewsbury and only one tunnel of significant length. The scenery too is very variable and whilst much can be enjoyed both from the lineside and train window, there are some features which can only be seen and fully appreciated when we move away from the railway altogether. For this reason I have purposely included a small number of pictures of some of the more outstanding places of interest served by the railway and which

are well worth visiting.

The whole of this Border country has a very long and complex historical background of which it has only been possible to give a very brief outline in this book. This likewise applies to the branch lines, more especially those in the coal mining areas of South Wales some of which, regrettably, have had to be omitted. But those which I have included give a fair coverage of the environment as a whole.

Acknowledgements

It is now my pleasant duty to express my thanks and appreciation to all who have, either directly or indirectly, contributed the many photographs contained in this album and whose names are credited beneath their respective pictures. Unfortunately I have not been able to use all of them and it has not been easy to decide which have had to be omitted. My aim has been to make the selection as varied as possible and the fact that a large number of them possess strong pictorial features has made my task all the more interesting and enjoyable.

I also wish to express my thanks to the following for their help in the preparation of this book:

Mr E. J. B. Stephens, Assistant Personnel Officer, BSC Stainless Panteg, for the aerial photograph showing the BSC Stainless Steel plant at Panteg, and also for introducing me to Mr J. S. Williams, a college lecturer of Griffithstown with a knowledge of local railway history and who, in turn updated me with detail of branch closures in the Eastern Valley and Pontypool districts.

Mr Seb Craig, Entertainments Manager, Shrewsbury and Atcham Borough Council, for photographs of Shrewsbury.

Mr Gerald A. Tuttum, Assistant Publicity Officer, Chester City Council for the loan of photographs of Chester.

Superintendent C. S. Boyle, West Mercia Constabulary, Ludlow, for kindly putting me into touch with Mr David Lloyd of Moseley, Birmingham who, in turn, provided historical information concerning Ludlow and Clee Hill.

Mr A. Jenkins of Orleton, Leominster also for up to date information relating to the Titterstone 'Dhu' stone quarries on Clee Hill.

Mr O. S. Nock for operational notes regarding the working of locomotives and travelling post office vehicles between the West of England and Crewe.

Mr W. G. Evans, Area Manager, British Rail (London Midland Region), Chester for historical notes relating to Shrewsbury station.

Mr Tony Rivers, Deputy Chairman, Great Western Society, for historical information concerning locomotive No 770, one of the '645' class of Wolverhampton built 0-6-0 saddle tank engines.

Messrs Ian Allan Ltd, for very kindly enabling me to peruse through their extensive library of railway photographs.

My many other friends too numerous to mention individually who have, in one way or another given me advice and information from which I have derived considerable benefit.

Finally, in search of additional material for this book, it has been a great pleasure to visit public libraries and peruse through the many publications and guides available — railway and non-railway alike. Appropriate references to these publications are given in the Bibliography.

C. R. L. Coles
Ruislip, Middlesex

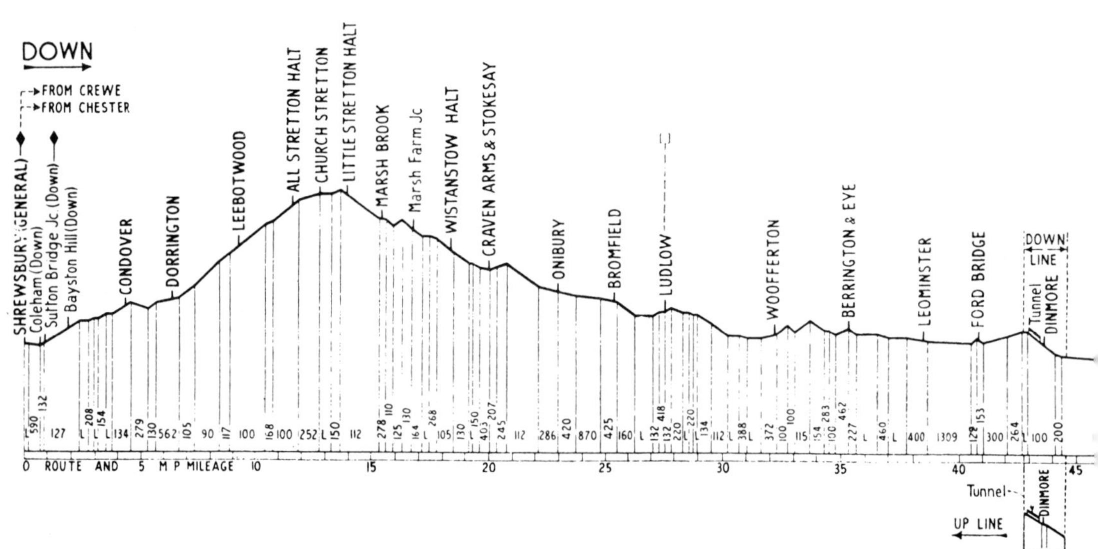

Introduction

For many centuries, bitter rivalry has existed between the peoples of England and Wales — this despite the fact that Christianity, which St Paul had already brought to Rome, had since become established in Britain during the second Roman occupation. Before they left in AD409, the Romans had, amongst other things, done much in the suppression of petty warfare. During the 5th and 6th centuries AD, the Anglo-Saxon conquest of Britain drove the Britons into the fastnesses of the western mountains and the Welsh people became their descendants. The country remained independent, under native princes, for the next 500 years until Edward I finally annexed Wales to the English Crown and gave to his infant son the title 'Prince of Wales'. From the year 1301 to this day, the heir to the English throne, if a male, has been styled as such. But tension between the two peoples erupted again during the reign of Henry IV when Owen Glendower, self-styled as a national hero and the last independent Prince of Wales, carried on what became the last war for Welsh independence. Although during Henry V's reign the Welsh were again subdued, it was not until 1536 during the reign of Henry VIII that, by an Act of Union passed by Parliament in that year, the Principality was finally and peaceably absorbed into the Tudor dynasty. Evidence of these campaigns can be seen today in what remains of the many feudal castles occupying strategic positions throughout the length and breadth of the Welsh Marches. Newport, Usk and Ludlow, these are names which will already be very familiar to those with a special interest in the former Great Western Railway.

Today the feeling of rivalry, though still keenly contested, especially in the fields of sport and art, is one of warmth and friendliness despite different customs of which, perhaps, that of language is in some areas most noticeable. Scenically, the whole area is one of contrasts from the somewhat drab industrial, yet busy, face of the environment in parts of the Black mountains to the more placid fruit growing areas in Herefordshire, and to the Shropshire hills — their heights extending to, in places, nearly 1,700ft above sea level. Nor must we omit the characteristic half-timbered style of building (wooden frames morticed together and fastened with wooden dowels), much of it dating back to the Tudor period — many examples of which are to be found in this part of England. The seasons too bring colour and character to the scene — pink and white fruit blossoms in spring contrasting with the cloth of autumn gold on the wooded slopes of the Long Mynd and Caer Caradoc, or winter's mantle of snow under which, on a bright crisp frosty day, the whole area can look serenely beautiful.

This then is the country through which, during the middle years of the last century, the main railway line as we know it today was constructed linking Newport with Shrewsbury thereby establishing connections with most other parts of Great Britain. Not the least interesting features of this line were the many branch lines giving access to the more isolated

Gradient profile showing the Shrewsbury-Newport section which is covered by the 'Welsh Marches Pullman' steam-hauled trains.

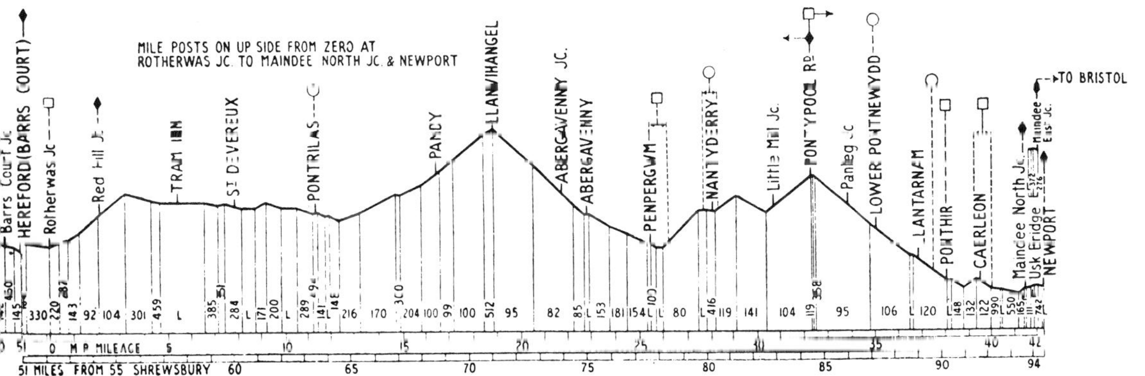

and little known outposts in the hills and valleys. For many years these lines provided the only contact with the outside world until they, in turn, were largely displaced by road transport. So much so that only the Central Wales line from Swansea and the Worcester to Hereford line remain operational today. Of the other 12 branches none survive apart from what is now preserved as the Severn Valley Railway and the odd short spur here and there, eg at Pontrilas.

Although the natural course along the river valleys is followed as much as possible, the North to West line abounds in a number of steep gradients — particularly in the region of Llanvihangel. In the steam era it was not infrequent for some of the more heavily loaded holiday expresses to be double-headed, or banked, over this part of the route. This brings me to the basic passenger service of today, which operates between Cardiff and Crewe. On summer Saturdays during the main holiday season, a

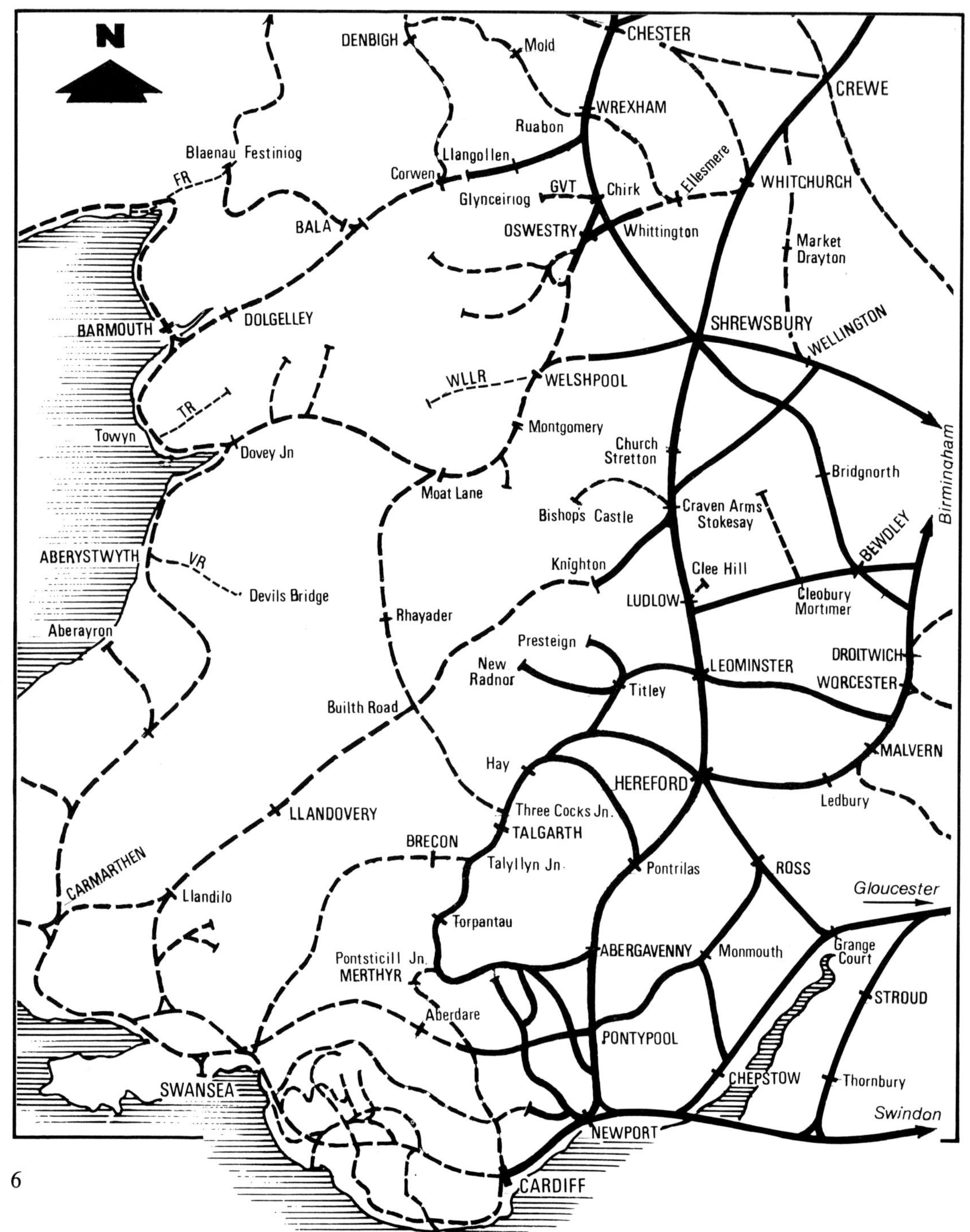

limited number of additional through trains run between the seaside resorts in Devon and Cornwall and Manchester (Piccadilly). During the steam era these through trains ran daily (including Sundays) during the summer to and from both Liverpool and Manchester. Some also conveyed through carriages to and from Scotland. Additional through trains also ran between Cardiff and Manchester. Train services were radically altered c1970 when most of the through trains were re-routed via the Lickey incline. Thus Cardiff would seem to be a very suitable starting point from which to pursue this journey northward — a journey full of imagination and recollection where the passage of time, extending over more than 75 years, is encompassed within the covers of this book. The many photographs which I have selected enable us to pause here and there as we proceed north, not only to re-live, in a sense, the pleasures of the clankity, clankity, clank rhythm of the carriage wheels as it traverses this branch or that one, but to familiarise ourselves with some little known, yet no less attractive, parts of the country.

Regarding train times, I have again elected to use both am/pm and the 24-hour clock especially as the period over which the many photographs were taken spreads over more than half a century. Where applicable the times in current use when the photographs were taken, if known, are included in the relevant captions. The pictures have been arranged in geographical sequence having regard to the numerous places en route as well as deviations here and there. Each, aided by its respective caption, endeavours to tell its own story.

The North to West line is one of those routes approved by British Rail on which steam-hauled special trains run at certain times of the year using preserved locomotives which have also been approved by British Rail. The 'Welsh Marches Pullman' is one such train which has run on a number of occasions during the last few years — usually south from Shrewsbury to Newport and back to Hereford and, less frequently, from Hereford to Chester and back to Shrewsbury. This is another reason why the $42\frac{1}{2}$ miles between Shrewsbury and Chester have been included — to say nothing of the added variety which this part of the route contributes to the overall railway scene. Because this album features the railway with emphasis being as much on the surrounding environment as on the trains themselves, I make no apologies at all for including several pictures featuring these specials — either as the principal subject, in differing locations, or as supporting interest where the dominant feature is of some other characteristic associated with the railway. Having set the scene, we now proceed to Cardiff and join the 12.45pm express for Manchester during the summer of 1951. The train is headed by 'Castle' class 4-6-0 locomotive No 5020 *Trematon Castle* (page 78).

Bibliography

Bangham, Peter E.; *A Regional History of the Railways of Great Britain, Volume II — North & Mid-Wales*; David & Charles Ltd, 1980.

Beck, Keith M.; *West Midland Lines of the GWR*; Ian Allan, 1983.

Bird, Vivian; *Exploring the West Midlands*; B. T. Batsford Ltd, 1977.

Fraser, Maxwell; *Welsh Border Country*; B. T. Batsford Ltd, 1972.

Handley, Brian; *The Wye Valley Railway*; Oakwood Press, 1982.

Harris, Michael; 'Three Partners in steam — the Hereford story', *Railway World*; September 1982.

Jenkins, Alfred; *Titterstone Clee Hills. Everyday Life, Industrial History and Dialect*; Orphans Printing Press and Studio Press, Birmingham, 1983.

Mais, S. P. B. and Stephenson, Tom (joint editors); *Lovely Britain*; Odhams Press Ltd, London.

Willward, Roy and Robinson, Adrian; *The Welsh Borders*; Eyre Methuen, 1978.

Nock, O. S.; *60 Years of Western Express Running*; Ian Allan Ltd, 1973.

Nock, O. S.; *The Great Western Railway. An Appreciation*; W. Heffer & Sons Ltd, Cambridge, 1951.

Pember, Geoffrey; 'An afternoon at Abergavenny Junction', *Railway World*; March 1983.

Rowley, Trevor; *The Shropshire Landscape*; Hodder & Stoughton, 1972.

Thomas, Roger; 'Britain's forgotten frontier', *In Britain*; June 1976.

Waite, Vincent; *Shropshire Hill Country*; J. M. Dent & Sons, 1970. Reprinted 1981 (paperback) by Phillmore & Co Ltd, London & Chichester.

British Rail Main Line Gradient Profiles, Ian Allan Ltd in collaboration with Tothill Press Ltd.

'The City of Chester', 'Chester Cathedral', 'Hereford Cathedral'; Pride of Britain paperback guides, published by Pitkin Pictorials Ltd.

Cardiff & Bristol to Hereford

It is but a short run from Cardiff to Newport to the west of which, at one time, a number of short distance branch lines converged. With their extremities more or less spread out in a northerly direction somewhat resembling the roots of a plant, these lines penetrated the valleys in the heart of the coal mining area of South Wales. Not all exist today and those that remain are now only used for the conveyance of coal from the pitheads. But first, we look at a trip up the Ebbw Valley to Abertillery close to which is Six Bells Colliery. Although about five miles west (as the crow flies) of the North to West main line, the overall scene here epitomises the general face of the environment in this part of the Welsh Marches.

Back then to Newport where we rejoin a northbound train which, on leaving the station, crosses the River Usk before taking the west curve of the Maindee triangle and continues in a northerly direction before re-crossing the river to follow the right bank as far as Caerleon — known as the *Isca Silurum of the Romans*. Here also are the remains of a Roman amphitheatre. Caerleon has also been claimed as being King Arthur's capital and the scene of the legendary Round Table. River and railway now part company — the latter turning westward to follow the valley of Afon Lwyd to Cwmbran and the industrial area between there and Pontypool. At Llantarnam the East Valley branch diverged from the main line to follow a near parallel course to Sebastopol where the nearby BSC stainless steel plant was sandwiched between the branch line on one side and the main line on the other side. Beyond Griffithstown the branch bore away leftwards to Abersychan and Blaenavon. This line is now closed — the last passenger train, the 'Welsh Collieries Rambler', ran on 13 April 1980. However the track was still *in situ* as recently as 30 October 1982 when another 'last train' hauled by Class 37 No 37.243 and bearing a placard with the legend 'Big Pit Special' became stuck en route to Furnace Sidings. Consisting of two coaches, wagons and a few tankers, this train had to be divided much to the delight of the photographers who had gathered to record this event. Apart from a section of track in the vicinity of Big Pit Museum, the whole of the East Valley branch has since been taken up.

Until in the 1960s, when many unprofitable branches were being closed, Pontypool Road station (now renamed Pontypool) could be a scene of much operational activity. The general layout included a marshalling yard and much siding accommodation for both passenger and freight vehicles. The station was also the junction for the Vale of Neath line which will be remembered by what was, without question, the most spectacular of all railway viaducts in this area — Crumlin, which was dismantled in 1967. Although this branch is now extinct, the stone-built viaduct further west near Hengoed was still intact at the end of 1982.

At one time most (if not all) of the west to north expresses called at Pontypool Road so it is now opportune that we should turn our attention to those routed via Bristol. Of these, the 8.45am from Plymouth to Manchester and the southbound counterpart were both worked between Newton Abbot and Shrewsbury without change of engine or crew. These duties were shared between the two depots. On some of the other expresses, eg relief trains during the summer season, engines were re-manned at Bristol. The mid-morning express from Plymouth (12.30pm ex-Bristol) conveyed a through carriage for Glasgow which was transferred at Crewe to the down 'Midday Scot'. But unquestionably the most interesting train of the day was the 12.10pm departure from Penzance which, prior to World War 2, conveyed a through portion for Glasgow the roofboards of which bore this legend: 'Glasgow Carlisle Crewe and the English Riviera'.

The stock was provided by the GWR who were very proud of these roofboards. This train, which also conveyed a TPO carriage from Plymouth, was invariably worked from Plymouth by a 'King' class 4-6-0 and was due at Bristol (Temple Meads) at approximately 7.00pm. Engines were changed here as, at that time, the 'King' class was not permitted to work through the Severn Tunnel. Meanwhile there was much cross-platform transfer of mail to the 7.20pm Midland TPO standing in platform 10. The Penzance (generally referred to as the 'mail') was also timed to depart from Bristol at the same time and, if both were running to schedule, they could often be seen leaving Temple Meads abreast of each other. At that time the 'mail' did not convey the Plymouth TPO beyond Bristol but it collected a Cardiff-Crewe TPO at Pontypool Road. During World War 2, when TPOs were suspended, the 7.30pm (as it then became) was worked from Bristol by a Salop engine but, with the reinstating of TPOs after the war, the working was changed — a Canton

'Castle' bringing the Cardiff-Crewe TPO to Pontypool Road where it awaited the arrival of the 'mail' from Bristol (usually worked by a 'Hall' class 4-6-0) which it then worked forward to Shrewsbury.

With the Usk valley on our right and the Black mountains to the left we continue, with a change to a downward gradient towards Abergavenny. Near Penpergwm the gradient again changes — continuing uphill to the summit at Llanvihangel — the steepest inclination being 1 in 82 over a distance of about two miles. Abergavenny is at the start of the steepest part of this incline and is a good centre from which to climb the Sugarloaf Mountain (1,955ft above sea level) which lies to the left as we approach the summit. On our right is a somewhat smaller height — Ysgyryd Fawr which rises to about 1,580ft above sea level. Both this and the Sugarloaf are owned by the National Trust. Beyond the Sugarloaf lie the Brecon Beacons now designated a National Park.

With a change of direction at Llanvihangel summit we now leave the Black mountains away to our left and, quickly gathering speed, head for the orchards and pastures of Herefordshire. What a blaze of colour if perchance our journey is made during blossom time on a sunny day with a clear blue sky above! What a contrast from the industrial face of the country now well behind us! At Pontrilas a short branch to our left to serve a nearby ordnance depot is all that remains of what at one time ran to Hay-on-Wye. Known as the Golden Valley line, it ceased to exist over 25 years ago.

The cathedral city of Hereford, supposedly the birthplace of Nell Gwynne, is the largest intermediate town on this part of the route and it is here that we make our first break of journey for there is much to see and enjoy. The square tower of the cathedral, which dominates the city, dates back to the 11th century. The cathedral contains a number of rare treasures of which, perhaps, the two most outstanding are the chained library and what is probably the oldest map of the world. Dating back to the 13th century it is known as the 'Mappa Mundi'. For those especially interested, the Pitkin pictorial guide, containing numerous photographs in colour and monochrome, is to be thoroughly recommended at its very modest price. The city grew round the cathedral and, with it, its trade, its industries (mainly rural) and its communications — rail and road.

Until the 1960s, Hereford was quite a busy railway centre. The junction for the Ledbury and Worcester line (shown on a GWR map as a major route), it was also the focal point for two branches. One was to Ross-on-Wye where this, too, diverged — left for Gloucester and right through the Wye Valley to Tydlnook (for the Forest of Dean lines) and Monmouth. Here there was yet another divergence — left for Tintern and Chepstow and right for Pontypool Road. These two lines formed

diversionary routes whenever essential maintenance work on the main line required complete track occupation — indeed, when the Severn Tunnel had to be closed, all through traffic to and from the west of England was re-routed via Gloucester.

The other branch from Hereford was to Three Cocks Junction where it joined the southern 'leg' of the former Cambrian Railways. It is of unusual interest in that, prior to the Grouping of 1923, it was part of the Midland Railway yet completely isolated, geographically, from its parent company. Today only the Worcester line remains open. All the other branches no longer exist apart from the odd building here and there for which fresh uses have been found. It is gratifying to note that the station and signalbox at Tintern have been converted into a countryside museum and administrative offices respectively.

As a railway centre, Hereford is but a shadow of the past. However, because of the generosity shown by Messrs H. P. Bulmer Ltd who have established what is now the Bulmer Railway Centre, a revival of interest and activity has taken place. This is largely due to the fact that three steam locomotives now based at this centre are among those approved by British Rail for working the periodic 'Welsh Marches Pullman'. Other 'approved' locomotives are those preserved by the Severn Valley Railway and work to and from Hereford via the Worcester line when occasion demands.

Lastly, before resuming our journey northwards, Hereford's close association with music is worth noting because there is a railway connection. The annual three choirs festival performed by the combined choirs of the cathedrals of Hereford, Worcester and Gloucester (and hosted in turn by these three cities), has been closely associated with one who is perhaps among the best loved of all English composers — Sir Edward Elgar whose oratorio 'The Dream of Gerontius' is traditionally performed every year on the final night of the festival. Hereford and the nearby Malvern Hills was Elgar's home country and it was in this city, during the year 1908, that he spent much time working on what has been acclaimed by many as being one of his greatest triumphs — Symphony No 1 in A flat major. In 1957, coincident with the centenary of the birth of Sir Edward Elgar and in recognition of his contribution to music, British Rail renamed 'Castle' class locomotive No 7005 *Lamphey Castle* after the great composer. For most of its working life, No 7005 was allocated to Worcester (85A) shed and not infrequently hauled the 'Cathedrals Express' between Hereford, Worcester and London. It was finally withdrawn from service in 1964.

To mark the 50th anniversary of Sir Edward Elgar's death BR decided to rename Class 50 No 50.007 after the composer, the unveiling being on 25 February 1984, performed by Simon Rattle. The locomotive is now in Brunswick green livery.

These three pictures, taken at Cardiff General c1922, will surely bring back memories of the true Great Western.
Above:
'Saint' class 4-6-0 No 2911 *Saint Agatha* alongside Manning Wardle 0-6-0ST *Phoenix*.
Right:
'Flower' class 4-4-0 No 4156 *Gardenia*.
Below right:
'County' class 4-4-0 No 3832 *County of Wilts.* See also p75.
All LCGB Ken Nunn Collection

Far right, top:
0-6-0ST No 770 taking water at Newport c1905. This locomotive was one of the '645' class which was built at Wolverhampton from 1873 onwards. No 770 was rebuilt at Swindon in 1925 as a pannier tank engine and withdrawn from service in October 1936 by which time it had covered a distance exceeding a million miles.
LCGB Ken Nunn Collection

Far right, bottom:
A Swansea-London express entering Newport station hauled by an unidentified 'Castle' class locomotive. *G. F. Heiron*

The Western Valley Branch

Top:
The branch from Newport to Brynmawr is now only used for goods traffic. Known as the Western Valley branch it follows the Ebbw Valley to Ebbw Junction where it divides — the left arm continuing to Ebbw Vale, and the right arm to Rose Heyworthy Colliery (two miles south of Brynmawr) where it now terminates. In this picture, taken on 5 January 1960, a three-car diesel unit forming the 11.17am train from Brynmawr to Newport is seen entering Risca station from which another branch (now extinct) deviated leftward to Nine Mile Point where it linked up with the former LNW Sirhowy Valley line from Nantybwch. *R. T. M. Hoyle*

Above:
A line-up of English Electric Class 37 diesel-electric locomotives at Ebbw Junction in February 1982. Since this photograph was taken, the allocation of motive power has been transferred to Severn Tunnel Junction.
Philip L. Williams

Top.
Heading towards Rose Heyworthy Colliery the 'Welsh Collieries Rambler' is here seen passing Aberbeeg on 13 April 1980. *Brian Morrison*

Above.
Block coal train leaving Six Bells Colliery (between four and five miles south of Rose Heyworthy Colliery) on 17 October 1968. *British Rail*

Newport to Pontypool

Above:
A Swansea-London IC125 train crossing the River Usk at Newport on 3 July 1977. *Dr L. A. Nixon*

Below:
Close-up view of the railway bridge spanning the River Usk at Newport. The train crossing the bridge is headed by 4-6-0 No 6000 *King George V* **and was photographed on 18 April 1981.** *Dr W. A. Sharman*

Above:
After turning on the Maindee triangle, 4-6-0 No 5051 *Drysllwyn Castle* **backs into Newport station on 16 April 1983 in readiness for working a northbound 'Welsh Marches Pullman'.** *Dr W. A. Sharman*

Below:
The 20.00 Cardiff-Crewe passenger and postal train, headed by English Electric Class 37 No 37.192, crossing the River Usk to the west bank, on the outskirts of Newport on a fine sunny evening in June 1981. *Peter J. C. Skelton*

Above:
Heralding the 'Return to Steam': 4-6-0 No 6000 *King George V* **approaching Caerleon with the Bulmers Cider train en route from Swindon to Hereford on 9 October 1971.** *Brian Stephenson*

Below:
North of Caerleon the railway turns westward and follows the Afon Lwyd (a tributary of the River Usk) as far as Pontypool. Pont-hir, where this picture was taken in March 1981, is about two miles north of Caerleon. Several spectators line the overbridge in the background as No 4930 *Hagley Hall* **passes a brickworks — almost completely obscured by the exhaust from the locomotive — as it heads northwards with a 'Welsh Marches Express'.** *J. S. Whiteley*

Above.
An aerial view of the Panteg Steel Works near Pontypool — sandwiched between the Eastern Valley branch to Blaenavon (left) and the main line (right). Pontypool town is to the upper left of the picture and the marshalling yard and locomotive depot at Pontypool Road (both no longer exist) can be seen in the top right hand corner. This picture was taken on 14 April 1959. *BSC Stainless Panteg*

Top left:
The 'Welsh Collieries Rambler', headed by English Electrics Class 37 locomotives Nos 37.179 and 37.182, photographed at Abersychan station on 13 April 1980. This was the last passenger train to travel over the branch to Blaenavon Colliery. *Brian Morrison*

Centre left:
The same train at Blaenavon Colliery. *Brian Morrison*

Below:
On 30 October 1982, under adverse weather conditions, Class 37 No 37.243 headed what was to be the last train to travel over the Eastern Valley branch — the 'Big Pit Special'. Consisting of two old coaches, some china clay wagons and a few tankers, the train had to be divided, because of the state of the track, and worked to Furnace Sidings in two parts. This picture, taken at Furnace Sidings, shows the second part of the train — now part of the Big Pit Mining Museum, which is located about one mile from Blaenavon Town. The museum, which was opened in spring 1983, includes the former coal washing buildings seen to the left of the locomotive. It is now under the care of the Torfean Museum Trust to whom it was handed over by the National Coal Board. *J. S. Williams*

Pontypool Road 1959-1982

Top right:
0-6-0PT No 4642, heading a southbound freight train, takes the avoiding line at Pontypool Road on 26 March 1959. *S. Rickard*

Centre right:
0-6-0PT No 3708 bringing a transfer freight train from the Northern sidings to Birkenhead sidings, Pontypool Road on 26 March 1959. In the background is Pontypool Road MPD.
S. Rickard

Below:
Pontypool Road — June 1982. Class 33 No 33.042 with a Crewe to Cardiff train is seen leaving the station (now known as Pontypool). The motive power depot, sidings and the platform awnings have all disappeared. *Colin J. Marsden*

Below:
'Saint' class 4-6-0 No 2920 *Saint David* at Bristol (Temple Meads) in June 1939 with a train for South Wales. The last survivor of the class, No 2920 spent the final years of its active existence in and around Hereford. With a shortage of serviceable motive power during World War 2, the surviving '29xx' class engines were not infrequently pressed into service on duties normally entrusted to 'Castle' class engines. Thus they became dubbed as the 'Hereford Castles'. *C. R. L. Coles*

Bottom:
The 12.10pm express from Penzance, which conveyed a through portion for Glasgow as well as a TPO from Plymouth, entering Bristol (Temple Meads) during the summer of 1939. The locomotive is 4-6-0 No 6022 *King Edward III*. *C. R. L. Coles*

Right:
'Star' class 4-6-0s Nos 4022 *Belgian Monarch* and 4045 *Prince John,* double-heading a west to north express, photographed in 1936 as they approached platform 8 at Bristol (Temple Meads). *C. R. L. Coles*

Centre right:
A year later at the same place — the corresponding train on this latter occasion being headed by 'Bulldog' class 4-4-0 No 3371 *Sir Massey Lopes* piloting an unidentified 'Hall' Class 4-6-0. *C. R. L. Coles*

Bottom right:
HST No 253.014 forming the 8.10 train from Paddington to Swanage passing Severn Tunnel junction on 15 July 1979. *Brian Morrison*

On the Vale of Neath Line

0-6-0PT No 3655 with a short westbound coal train
coming off the stone viaduct near Hengoed High Level
station. Although this part of the line has been closed for
some years, the viaduct was still intact in November 1982
— crossing the valley up which the Newport to Brecon line
at one time followed. *R. E. Toop*

Crumlin viaduct carried the Vale of Neath line across the Ebbw Valley up which the Western Valley branch runs to Rose Heyworth Colliery. This viaduct was dismantled in 1967. *British Rail*

Below:
Manchester to Plymouth express headed by rebuilt 'Royal Scot' 4-6-0 No 46143 *The South Staffordshire Regiment* **passing Penpergwm, south of Abergavenny on 18 July 1958.** *D. S. Fish*

Bottom:
4-6-2 No 46229 *Duchess of Hamilton* **at the head of a northbound 'Welsh Marches Pullman' photographed near Abergavenny in October 1982.** *D. Cobbe*
D. Cobbe

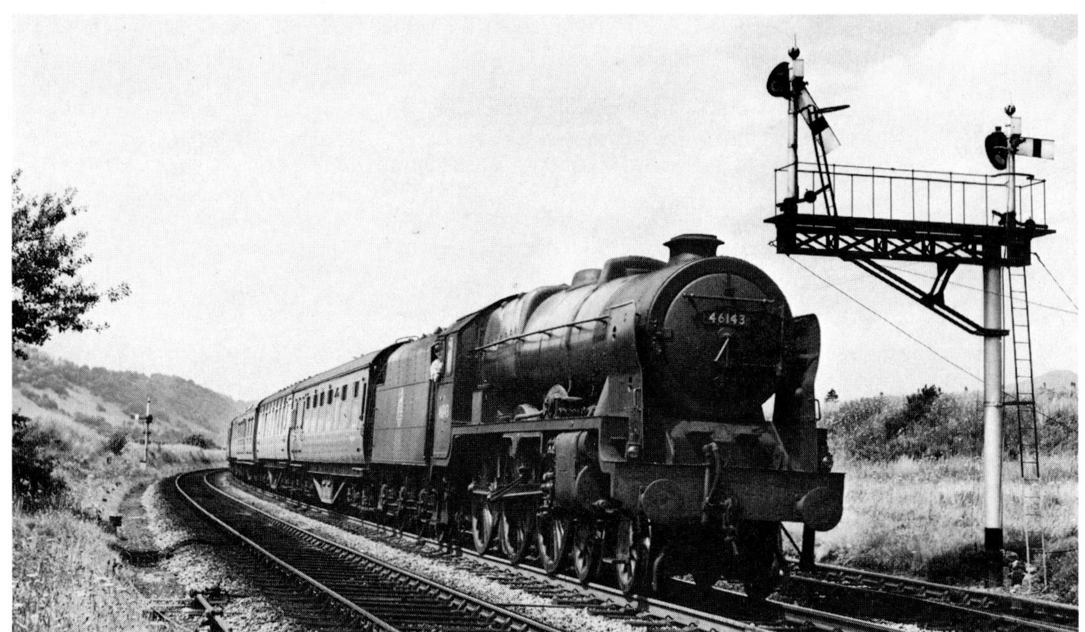

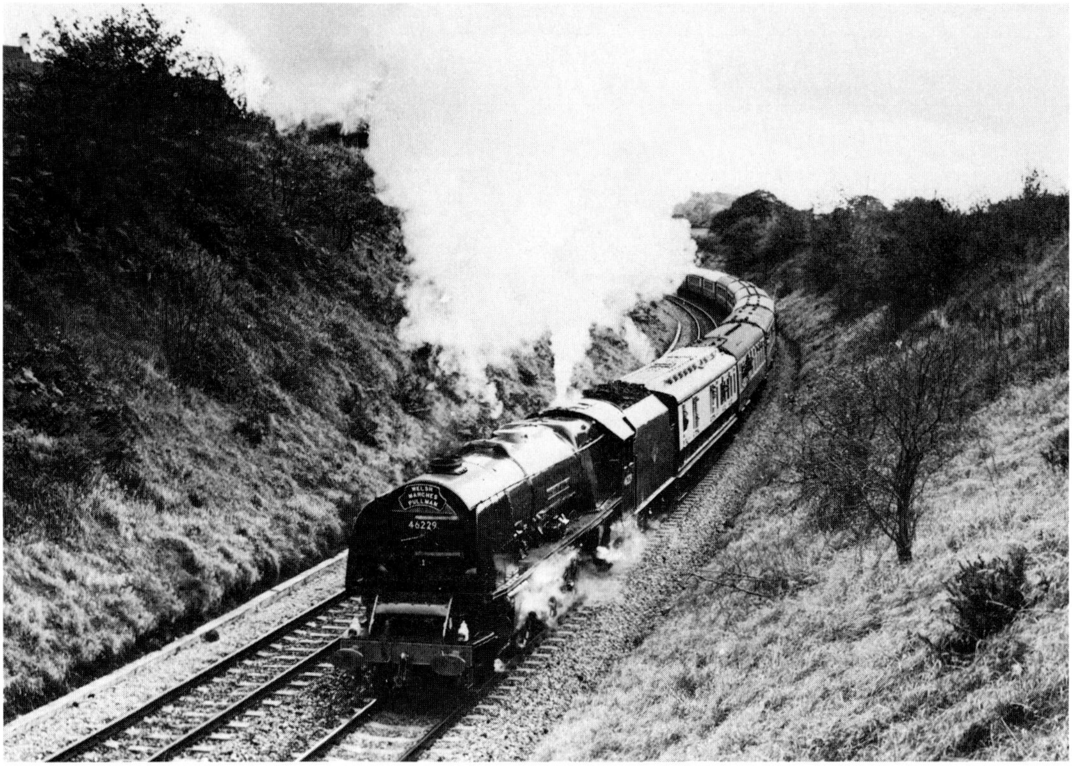

Below:
Once again, and for the last time on our journey northward, we cross the River Usk (also known as the Afon Wysg) south of Abergavenny at a point known as The Bryn. On this occasion, 4-6-0 No 7812 *Erlestoke Manor* piloting No 4930 *Hagley Hall* is heading a northbound Welsh Marches Pullman towards Abergavenny on 17 April 1982. (See also page 32).
Peter J. C. Skelton

Bottom:
In the same locality, Class 33 No 33.019 heads a Cardiff to Crewe train in June 1982. *Colin J. Marsden*

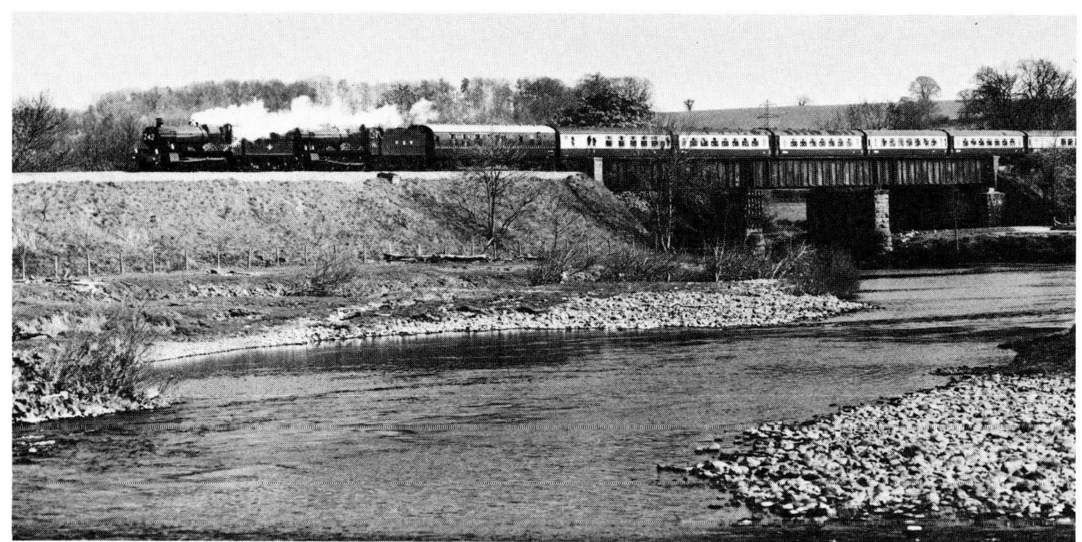

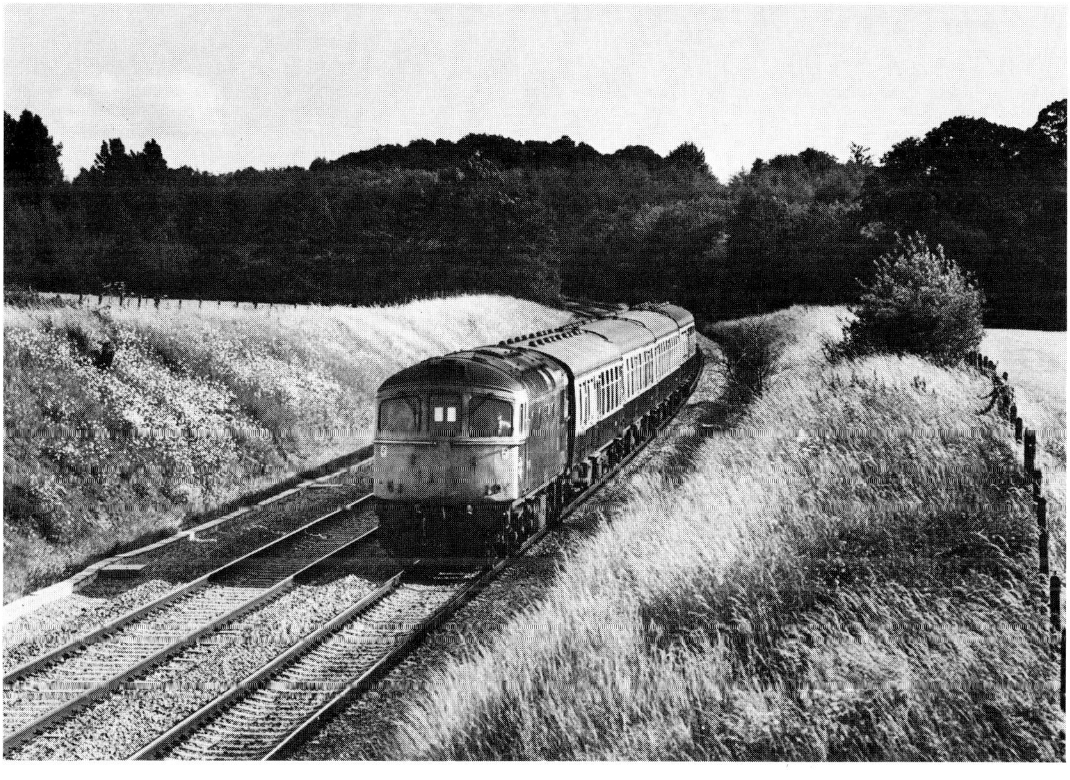

Above:
Impact indeed! Heavy skies and a gleam of low angle contra-jour lighting have created this strikingly pictorial impression of No 6201 *Princess Elizabeth* **heading north with a 'Welsh Marches Pullman' near Abergavenny on 30 January 1982.** *Peter. J. C. Skelton*

Below:
At Abergavenny station on 31 October 1982 when Class 37 No 37.302 was crossing to the southbound track with a PW train. *Dr W. A. Sharman*

Above:
The southbound 'Welsh Dragon' approaching Abergavenny on 11 October 1980 hauled by preserved Class 5 4-6-0 No 5000 piloting Ivatt 2-6-0 No 43106. The Sugarloaf mountain provides background scenery.
Peter J. C. Skelton

The LNWR at Abergavenny

Above:
At Abergavenny junction a branch line — prior to 1923 part of the LNWR — extended westward to Dowlais (where it linked up with the Newport to Brecon line). This picture, taken on 3 May 1951 at Brynmawr station (terminal point of the GW Western Valley branch), shows ex-LNWR 0-8-0 No 49403 with a freight train for Abergavenny. *R. C. Riley*

Below:
Nantybwch station was further west. Here a former L&YR two-coach train was being loaded with parcels on the same day. *R. C. Riley*

Above right:
The evening freight train from Abergavenny Junction to Brynmawr crossing the River Usk at Abergavenny in charge of ex-LNWR 0-8-0 No 49226 in September 1952. *P. M. Alexander*

Below right:
A pre-Grouping scene at Abergavenny Junction c1920 with ex-LNWR Webb 0-6-2T No 435 piloting sister engine No 1358 on a passenger special. This station was closed for passenger traffic during 1958. *Real Photos (42111)*

On Llanvihangel Bank

Above, Below:
2-6-0 No 6361 photographed on 1 June, 1953 with a northbound goods train, assisted (below) in the rear by 2-6-2T No 40145. At this point the gradient varies between 1 in 82/95 facing northbound trains. *R. C. Riley*

Above:
With the Sugarloaf mountain in the background, 0-8-0
No 49028 coasts down the gradient towards Abergavenny
with a loose-coupled freight train in June 1953.
R. C. Riley

Below:
The Sugarloaf mountain dominates the scene as Class 33
No 33.026 heads south near Triley Mill with the 12.25
train from Crewe to Cardiff on 24 August 1982.
Dr W. A. Sharman

Above:
4-6-0s Nos 7812 *Erlestoke Manor* **and 4039** *Hagley Hall* **climbing Llanvihangel Bank near Triley Mill with a 'Welsh Marches Pullman' on 17 April 1982. (See also page 25).** *David Hunt*

Below:
Llanvihangel station (now closed) was at the summit of the 1 in 82/95 drag from Abergavenny. A northbound coal train hauled by 2-8-0 No 3803 is here seen passing through the station on 18 May 1957 with the slopes of the Black mountains behind. *Geoffrey F. Bannister*

Above:
A glorious spring day heralds a fine performance by single-chimneyed 4-6-0 No 5051 *Drysllwyn Castle* **when approaching the summit of Llanvihangel bank with the southbound 'Welsh Marches Pullman' on 16 April 1983.**
Peter J. C. Skelton

Below:
Approaching Llanvihangel summit from the north. 2-6-0 No 5378 piloting 2-8-0 No 2841 heading a freight train for South Wales on 13 September 1952. At this point the gradient facing southbound trains is 1 in 100.
P. M. Alexander

Pandy to Hereford

A picturesque scene near Pandy where the railway keeps close company with the River Monnow. 2-10-0 No 92220 *Evening Star* is here seen at the head of a southbound 'Welsh Marches Pullman' on 24 May 1982.
Peter J. C. Skelton

Above:
A little further north, the contours of the Black mountains provide the background scene as 4-6-0 No 5000 heads south on a similar duty on 13 March 1982.
Peter J. C. Skelton

Below:
'N15' class 4-6-0 No 777 *Sir Lamiel*, resplendent in Southern green livery, is here seen south of Pontrilas at the head of the southbound 'Welsh Marches Pullman' on 9 April 1983. *Peter J. C. Skelton*

No 92220 photographed at Pontrilas on the return journey to Hereford with a 'Welsh Marches Pullman' on 24 May 1982. *Dr L. A. Nixon*

Above:
An unidentified 'Warship' Class 4 diesel-hydraulic locomotive, heading the 9.5am express from Liverpool, passing the then disused Pontrilas station on 27 June 1963. *Anthony A. Vickers*

Below:
The golden valley branch line to Hay-on-Wye, which diverged from the main line near Pontrilas became extinct with the closing of the last section from Abbey Dore to Pontrilas in June 1957. This picture shows Westbrook station, five stops further up the branch, as it appeared on 6 July 1958 — track lifted and since overgrown with the level crossing gates permanently 'open' for road traffic. *H. C. Casserley*

Above:
It is blossom time as we head north past the Herefordshire orchards towards St Devereux. A view from the footplate of 4-6-0 No 2938 *Corsham Court* **taken during the early 1950s.** *R. C. Riley*

Below:
On 30 January 1982, the 'Welsh Marches Pullman' was headed by No 6201 *Princess Elizabeth,* **here seen on the southbound run near St Devereux.** *Peter J. C. Skelton*

Variety at Hereford

Above:
Collett 0-6-0 No 2249 on a southbound stopping train
leaving Hereford on 18 August 1962.   *R. C. Riley*

Below.
North to west express near Hereford headed by rebuilt
'Royal Scot' 4-6-0 No 46160 *Queen Victoria's Rifleman'*
— 18 August 1962.   *R. C. Riley*

Above:

On shed at Hereford on 17 May 1952. 4-6-0 No 46118 *Royal Welch Fusilier* **and unidentified ex-GWR '28xx' class 2-8-0.** *R. C. Riley*

Below:

Hereford station on 31 March 1981. No 6000 *King George V*, **which had worked the 'Welsh Marches Express' from Shrewsbury, comes off the train in exchange for No 4930** *Hagley Hall* **(in background) which hauled the train to Newport.** *Dr W. A. Sharman*

Above:
Repeat performance two years later but with a different cast — the two principal 'characters' on 16 April 1983 being *Sir Lamiel* and *Drysllwyn Castle*.
Graham Scott-Lowe

Above:
At the conclusion of duty on a 'Welsh Marches Pullman' 4-6-0s Nos 5000 and 4930 proceed to Bulmers Yard, Hereford on 20 March 1982 before returning to the Severn Valley Railway. *Dr W. A. Sharman*

Below:
An open day at the Bulmer Railway Centre, Hereford.
R. O. Conway

Above:
The medieval bridge carrying the A49 road over the River Wye at Hereford with the cathedral in the background. *D. E. Edwards*

Right:
The 'Old House' in Hereford is an early 17th century timber-framed building — the advantage of this form of construction being its portability. During the 1960s, this house, now a museum, was dismantled and re-erected on its present site. The interspaces between the timbers are filled with wattle-and-daub and plastered over. We shall meet up with other examples of this type as we continue our journey northward. *D. E. Edwards*

Left and below:
'Castle' class locomotive No 7005 renamed *Sir Edward Elgar* undergoing repair at Worcester. This very popular engine often hauled the 'Cathedrals Express' between Hereford and London.
Geo Osborne (upper), South Devon Railway Museum (below)

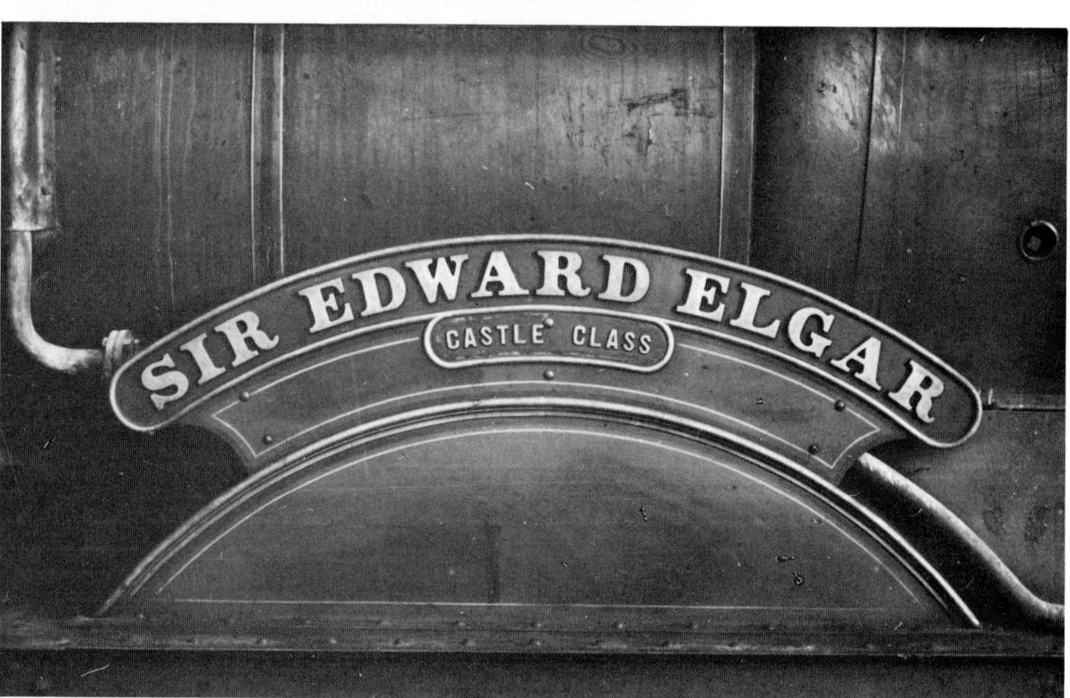

Above:
4-6-0s Nos **7812** *Erlestoke Manor* and **4930** *Hagley Hall* on the line between Worcester and Hereford near Ledbury, en route from the Severn Valley Railway prior to working a 'Welsh Marches Express' in April 1982. *Dr L. A. Nixon*

Below:
The line from Hereford to Shrewsbury was, before the Grouping in 1923, jointly owned by the GWR and LNWR. It was opened in December 1853 thereby enabling through traffic to operate between Newport and Shrewsbury — the section south of Hereford having been completed seven years earlier. *C. R. L. Coles*

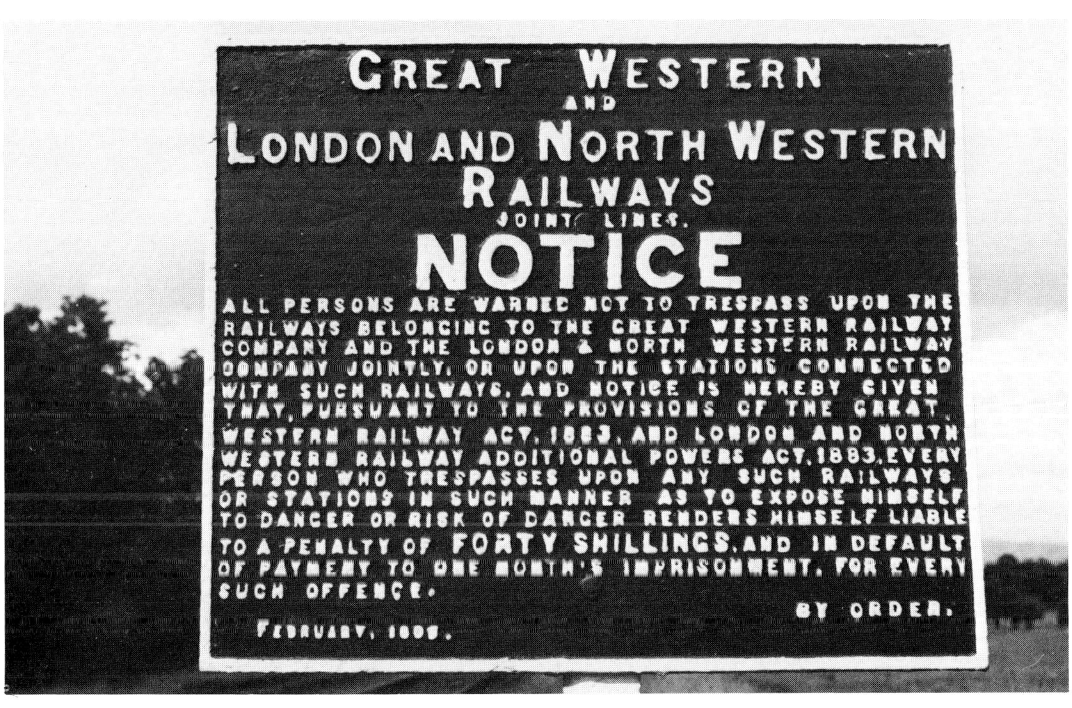

From Hereford to Pontsticill Junction

Above:
Ivatt 2-6-0 No 46510, heading the 12.42pm from Hereford to Brecon, passing on to the Brecon branch at Barton Curve, Hereford on 1 May 1962. The purpose of the route indicator signal in the foreground is not apparent and it was not observed. Nor was there any indication that it was inoperative. *Anthony A. Vickers*

Left:
Collett 0-6-0 No 2287 with the thrice weekly branch freight train from Eardisley passing Moorhampton on 9 September 1964. This service was withdrawn a month later and the branch completely closed. *E. J. S. Gadsden*

Top right:
2-6-0 No 78004 with a Hereford to Brecon goods train at Moorhampton on 23 April 1958.
H. C. Casserley

Centre right:
Ex-L&YR 0-6-0 No 12551 on a train from Three Cocks Junction to Hereford photographed at Eardisley on 9 September 1949. This branch was closed to passenger traffic in 1962.
H. C. Casserley

Below:
Three Cocks Junction station. The train headed by Ivatt 2-6-0 No 46508 is the then 1.25pm from Brecon to Moat Lane (former Cambrian Railways) and was photographed on 28 July 1959. The station buildings here are now used by a bottle gas company.
R. O. Tuck

Above:
The 12.15pm Hereford to Dowlais Central empty tanker train headed by 0-6-0PT No 3728 waiting for the road through to Tal-y-Llyn at Talgarth station (former Cambrian Railways) on 28 July 1959. It was a regular working of ammonia tankers to and from ICI Dowlais. This, the southern end of what was once known as the Mid-Wales Railway (which was later bought out by the Cambrian Railways), was closed in 1962. *R. O. Tuck*

Centre left:
Scene at Tal-y-Llyn Junction on 3 May 1951 with an ex-Cambrian Railways 0-6-0 No 849 on a train off the Mid-Wales line from Moat Lane. Before 1923 the continuation southward was part of the Brecon and Merthyr Railway. *R. C. Riley*

Bottom left:
Cambrian Railways cast iron warning notice. Brief — but to the point. *C. R. L. Coles*

Above:
At Pontsticill Junction (five stations south of Tal-y-Llyn Junction), the line again divided — right for Merthyr and left for Dowlais. Before these rural branch lines were closed during the 1960s, it was possible to return to Abergavenny Junction over the former LNW branch from Dowlais, or to Newport via the Sirhowy Valley line. This picture was taken in 1951. *R. C. Riley*

Below:
The Brecon Beacons (now a National Park) with, in the middle distance, the Pontsticill reservoir, provide the setting for this picturesque scene on the narrow gauge (1ft $11\frac{1}{2}$in) Brecon Mountain Railway. This line operates over a distance of two miles between Pant and Pontsticill. The train is headed by 0-6-2WT No 99.3353 *Graf Schwerin Lowitz* which was built in 1908 by Arn Jung (1261), East Germany. *Mike Floate*

Above:
The branch from Hereford to Ross-on-Wye crossed the River Wye in three places. In this picture an unidentified GWR 4-6-0 is seen crossing the river at Backney with an afternoon Hereford to Gloucester train in September 1964 — less than two months before the branch was closed.
E. J. S. Gadsden

50

Above:
2-6-2T No 4124 at Ross-on-Wye on 28 July 1961 heading the 2.08pm train from Gloucester to Hereford.
F. K. Davies

Below:
BR Standard 2-6-4T No 80100 awaits departure from Mitcheldean Road station, on the northern edge of the Forest of Dean, with an afternoon Gloucester to Hereford train in September 1964. No 80100 is at present in process of being restored by the Bluebell Railway at Sheffield Park. *E. J. S. Gadsden*

Above:
Plymouth to Liverpool express, double-headed by 2-6-0s Nos 7332 and 6378, emerging from the north west portal of Lea Tunnel under adverse weather conditions on 11 March 1962. Because of PW repairs in the Severn Tunnel at that time, all traffic between Hereford and the West of England was being diverted via Gloucester and Ross-on-Wye. *B. J. Ashworth*

Centre left:
The 14.38 train from Hereford to Gloucester, headed by 2-6-0 No 7319, emerging from Lea tunnel on 22 June 1964.
B. J. Ashworth

Bottom left:
Diverted trains between Hereford and the West of England used the former Midland Railway main line between Gloucester and Bristol. In this picture, taken in June 1964, Stanier '8F' 2-8-0 No 48005 is seen passing Haresfield with a southbound goods train en route for Bristol. *E. J. S. Gadsden*

Above:
The branch between Ross-on-Wye and Monmouth crossed the River Wye at Kerne Bridge. In this picture, taken on 2 September 1964, 0-6-0 No 2286 is crossing this bridge with the return freight from Lydbrook Junction to Ross-on-Wye. *E. J. S. Gadsden*

Top:
Lydbrook was the junction for the short branches to terminal points in the Forest of Dean. 0-6-0 No 2286 is seen standing at the station with a short goods train on 2 September 1964. The adjoining cable works, hence the empty cable drums by the station platform, was the main reason why the line between here and Ross-on-Wye was among the last of the Wye Valley branches to remain open (if only for goods traffic) until it, too, was closed later in that year. *E. J. S. Gadsden*

Above:
Monmouth Troy station looking west in April 1931. Here there was yet another junction — trains proceeding either to Pontypool Road (via Usk) or to Chepstow (via Tintern). *H. C. Casserley*

Above right:
Although passenger trains over the Wye Valley branch south of Ross-on-Wye were withdrawn in January 1959, the line remained open for goods traffic for a further five years after which it was completely closed and the track subsequently lifted. This picture of Redbrook-on-Wye station was taken in November 1970 by which time an abundance of natural vegetation had become firmly established. *South Devon Railway Museum*

Right:
The 11.30 train from Gloucester to Newport approaching Chepstow on 12 April 1980. *Brian Morrison*

54

Hereford to Shrewsbury

The 51 miles from Hereford to Shrewsbury were jointly owned by the GWR and LNWR (later LMS). The LNWR also exercised running powers over the GWR line south of Hereford thus enabling them to reach their own branch from Abergavenny Junction to Dowlais.

About three miles north of Shelwick Junction, where the Worcester line swings to the right, a short branch leaves the main line on the left and, following a parallel course for a brief distance, bears away left to serve a government establishment at Moreton-on-Lugg. Leominster is the next sizeable town north of Hereford and was the junction of two branches — to Titley (from which spurs extended to New Radnor, Presteign and Eardisley, where contact was made with the Midland Railway's branch from Hereford to Three Cocks Junction) and eastward to Bromyard and Worcester. Neither exist today.

During the English-Welsh campaigns of the middle ages, Leominster was a frontier town directly involved in the fighting. It is said that it was founded by Leofric, husband of Lady Godiva. It later became famous as a wool marketing centre — the fine rich fleeces it produced becoming known as 'Leominster Ore'. East of Leominster is one of the hop-growing districts of Herefordshire and where the sight of hop-poles and oast houses is reminiscent of parts of Kent.

We are now approaching what has been described elsewhere as the loveliest run of all, mainly on a noticeable yet not steep rising gradient which remains virtually unbroken until the summit is reached near Church Stretton. As we pass through Leominster we may catch a glimpse of the black and white timbered dwellings characteristic of this part of the country and of which more later. After Woofferton, once the junction for the now extinct branch to Tenbury Wells and Kidderminster, we follow the valley of the River Teme and keep in close proximity with the river until, approaching Ludlow, river and railway part company, the former circling round the west of the town whilst the railway continues in a more northerly direction. Ludlow is a most attractive English market town and its castle, the most important of the many Border castles, surpasses all others both in size and in its records of chivalry and fierce warfare. The town itself stands on a hill and the tower of the Parish church of St Lawrence is a landmark for many miles around.

Here we again break our journey for a look round the town and also to visit the mineral line on nearby Clee Hill before continuing to Shrewsbury.

Beyond Ludlow and about a mile south of Onibury, the railway meets up with the River Onny, a tributary of the Teme, and both keep in close company as far as Stokesay Castle — a fortified manor house dating back to the Tudor period and still inhabited today. O. S. Nock has described the view from the train as 'one of the choicest scenes on the Welsh border'. Trevor Rowley, in his book *The Shropshire Landscape* goes even further and describes Stokesay Castle with the nearby church as 'one of the most perfect pictures of rural serenity in Britain'.

Soon we approach Craven Arms, junction for the Central Wales line which joins us from the left. Ahead, the valley narrows with the Long Mynd on our left and along the crest of which is the track of the 'Port Way' — built by the Romans. Stretford Bridge, a mile north of Craven Arms was once the junction for the almost forgotten Bishops Castle Light Railway. With a length of $10\frac{1}{2}$ miles, this railway was one of a number which, during the present century, came under the management of Lt-Col H. F. Stephens. It is on record that it was never out of debt and, in 1877, the bailiffs moved in — for the second time since the line first opened in 1865. On this latter occasion they removed a rail and erected a fence across the track on ground near Horderley — the railway not having paid for this piece of land. Operationally it was a curious system — trains running from Craven Arms to Lydham Heath where reversal was necessary to reach the terminus at Bishops Castle. At the time of closure in April 1935, the railway was already in the hands of an official receiver. However, the rails received a new lease of life when subsequently taken to Cammel Laird's shipyard on the Mersey where they were used in the stocks for building HMS *Prince of Wales* — the ill-fated battleship sunk by the Japanese off Malaya in December 1941. It will be recalled that, earlier in the year, HMS *Prince of Wales* had been engaged in the naval action in the Denmark Strait (between Iceland and Greenland) which culminated in the sinking of the German battleship *Bismarck* on the morning of 27 May 1941.

About $2\frac{1}{2}$ miles further north we pass the site of Marsh Farm Junction from which the Much Wenlock branch diverged to the right. Keeping in close company with Wenlock Edge on our right, the clankity-clank, characteristic of many branch lines, recalls A. E. Houseman's poem *A Shropshire Lad* — a musical arrangement for which (tenor voice, piano and string quartet) was composed by Ralph Vaughan Williams:

On Wenlock Edge the wood's in trouble,
His forest fleece the Wrekin heaves;
The gale, it plays the saplings double,
And thick on Severn snow the leaves.

This branch also played host to HM Queen Elizabeth II when, in October 1952 during her visit to Shropshire to open the Claerwen Dam, the Royal Train was stabled overnight close to Harton Road station. At that time the branch had already been closed to passenger traffic — the last train running in December 1951.

Back on the main line as we approach Church Stretton— the summit of this long drag from Hereford — we meet up with and keep close company with another Roman road (Watling Street) on our right and beneath the slopes of Caer Caradoc. With a falling gradient after Church Stretton and speed accelerating, we soon get our first glimpse of the many church spires of the old Border town of Shrewsbury — once another of the many frontier posts in the forefront during the campaigns of the 15th century. Here we alight because the train from Hereford continues to Crewe where, should it be conveying a through portion for Scotland, this would be transferred to one or other of the principal Anglo-Scottish expresses — an operation of which very little is seen in Great Britain today though, of necessity, it is widespread on the European mainland. Shrewsbury can still be regarded as a major railway centre from which five routes radiate like the points of a compass. At one time there existed a sixth line — the branch to Bewdley and Kidderminster, part of which, south of Bridgnorth, is now preserved as the Severn Valley Railway.

This part of Shropshire witnessed the birth of the Industrial Revolution in the 18th century — the cradle of which, Coalbrookdale, lies about 10 miles southeast of Shrewsbury. Abraham Darby, Thomas Telford and, a little later, Richard Trevithick were amongst the pioneers of this enterprise — today kept alive by the Ironbridge Gorge Museum, covering an area of six square miles, and opened in 1973. Darby's iron bridge, one of the most striking monuments of this age, has spanned the Severn gorge since 1779. Further downstream the Victoria Bridge, dating from 1861, carries the Severn Valley Railway across the river in a 200ft span of cast iron. This bridge was also cast at the Coalbrookdale Company's works — the work being engineered by John Fowler who, it will be recalled, later became one of the architects of the Forth Bridge.

Of Scottish descent, Telford specialised in the construction of canals and road making. His principal contribution to the Industrial Revolution was in 1796 when he built the first cast-iron aqueduct to carry the Shrewsbury Canal across the Tern Valley at Longdon-on-Tern — a distance of 62yd. Later, Telford moved to Shrewsbury to convert the castle into a residence and whilst there he was appointed Surveyor of Public Works for Shropshire. Telford was followed early in the 19th century by Trevithick, a native of Cornwall and father of steam locomotion, whose first locomotive was produced at Coalbrookdale. A few years later, in 1808, Trevithick's *Catch Me Who Can* engine was built at Hazeldine Foundry close to the River Severn at Bridgnorth.

Shrewsbury is without doubt the most historical of all the towns we have, so far, either passed through or visited and we may as well spend a few hours here before continuing to Chester. As we pass by the Abbey Church which was founded in 1083, and continue along Abbey Foregate towards the English Bridge, we may recall that it was here, under the very shadow of the abbey, that the terminus of the one-time Shropshire and Montgomeryshire Light Railway was located. This line diverged from the Shrewsbury-Welshpool line and ran to Criggion Quarry. The bridge over the River Severn near Melverley, which once carried the track, has since been paved as a road bridge and marks the boundary between England and Wales. This small light railway will best be remembered by what must surely be the smallest steam locomotive ever to run on standard gauge track. In later years the railway was taken over by the Royal Engineers who, after using it for a while, preserved this diminutive 0-4-2 engine (named *Gazelle*) and eventually brought it to the Longmoor Military Railway where it was positioned on a short length of track. Restored in the livery of the Royal Corps of Transport, *Gazelle* was presented to the National Railway Museum in 1975 since when it has been transferred to the recently established Museum of Army Transport on Humberside where it is one of the standard gauge railway exhibits.

As we return back to the railway station, one of many buildings listed for preservation by the Department of the Environment, we are reminded that the eminent biologist, Charles Darwin, was born in Shrewsbury in 1809. Darwin is best remembered for his researches into the origin of the many millions of different kinds of species of living beings with which Nature fills the whole universe. He died in April, 1882 and is buried among Britain's greatest in Westminster Abbey. In 1982, to mark the centenary of Darwin's death, the Post Office issued a set of four commemorative stamps depicting some of his researches.

But now we must hurry or else we shall miss the next train to Chester.

4-6-0 No 850 *Lord Nelson* **leaving Hereford for Shewsbury with the SLOA 'Cathedrals Pullman' on 13 June 1981.** *J. S. Whiteley*

Above:
Class 40 diesel-electric locomotive No 40.106, painted in the earlier BR green livery, photographed from the same place on 13 March 1982 with a 'Welsh Marches Express' en route for Shrewsbury and Crewe. This locomotive has since been withdrawn from service. *J. S. Whiteley*

Above right:
No 4472 *Flying Scotsman* **about to enter Dinmore tunnel with a railway enthusiasts' special on 6 April 1974.** *R. E. B. Siviter*

Right:
At the north end of Dinmore tunnel, Class 47 diesel-electric No 47.076 *City of Truro* **emerges with an oil freight train for Ellsmere Port on 5 June 1982. (See also page 82.)** *Dr W. A. Sharman*

58

CATCH POINTS
LNER
FLYING SCOTSMAN

Above:
Leominster was the junction for the Eardisley, New Radnor and Presteign branches. It was also the junction for the Bromyard line. This picture, taken on 24 July 1951 showing the station nameboard indicates that, at that time, passenger services were still in operation on the Bromyard branch but extended no further than Kington on the other branches. *R. C. Riley*

Below:
No 47.076 *City of Truro,* **hauling failed Class 40 No 40.126 and a rake of oil tankers, passes through Leominster station in June 1982 as passengers await their train.** *Dr W. A. Sharman*

Above:
Rowden Mill station as in May 1952. The whole of this branch (Leominster-Bromyard-Worcester) is now extinct.
H. C. Casserley

On the New Radnor and Presteign Branches

Below:
Picturesque Kingsland, with its flower beds and roses, was the first station on the branch from Leominster. This picture was taken in July 1951. *R. C. Riley*

Above:
At Titley Junction the line split into three different directions — to Eardisley, New Radnor and Presteign. In this picture 0-4-2T No 1420 heads the return freight from Presteign to Kington shortly before closure in September 1964. Of particular note is the abundance of natural vegetation on both track and platforms — the branch having been closed for passenger traffic since February 1955. *E. J. S. Gadsden*

Below:
A truly rural level crossing, complete with wicket gate and warning notice. No 1420, photographed at Pembridge on the same day as the picture above. *E. J. S. Gadsden*

Right:
Kington station as on 24 July 1951. *R. C. Riley*

Below right:
0-4-2T No 1413 approaching Kington station with a push and pull train on 5 February 1955 — the last day on which this branch was open for passenger traffic. *Donald Kelk*

Top:
0-4-2T No 1420 sets off from Presteign in September 1964 with a lightweight freight to return to Kington and Leominster. *E. J. S. Gadsden*

Above:
On the New Radnor branch in July 1957, 0-4-2T No 1455 with a SLS special pauses for a photographic stop at Dolyhir station. Regular passenger services on this branch were withdrawn on 5 February 1951 — the line finally closing on 9 June 1958. *R. M. Casserley*

Above right:
Back on the main line at what was then Woofferton Junction. This picture, taken on 10 June 1957, shows 0-6-0PT No 4641 arriving at the station with the 6.25pm train from Kidderminster. The train in the right foreground is the then 6.25pm from Shrewsbury to Hereford with which the branch train made connection. This branch is now extinct. *M. Mensing*

Right:
Churchward 2-8-0 No 2822 near Woofferton Junction in June 1951 with a northbound freight train. *C. R. L. Coles*

Above:
Austerity 2-8-0 No 90579 passing Ashford Bowdler with a northbound freight train in June 1951. *C. R. L. Coles*

West to north express (4.30pm ex-Bristol Temple Meads) passing Ashford Bowdler in June 1951 hauled by 4-6-0 No 7034 *Ince Castle*. *C. R. L. Coles*

Welcome to Ludlow

Top:
Ludlow, with Dinham Bridge in the foreground, as seen from Whitcliffe Hill. This view has been described as one of the finest in England. The railway passes to the right of the town. Ludlow Castle is on the left of the picture whilst, to the right of the church is Clee Hill up which, until 1962, a mineral railway served the Titterstone Granite Quarries. *C. R. L. Coles*

Above:
Picturesque Ludford Bridge, which dates back to the 15th century, with its deep V-shaped nitches for use by pedestrians, carries the A49 road across the River Teme. It is only wide enough for one lane of traffic the flow of which is controlled by colour light signals. This route through Ludlow is now bypassed. *C. R. L. Coles*

68

Top:
Looking down Broad Street from the buttermarket.
C. R. L. Coles

Above left:
A contra-jour study in one of Ludlow's picturesque narrow Tudor passageways — Church Street. *C. R. L. Coles*

Above right:
The 'Rose & Crown' Inn, a very attractive half-timbered building, was first licensed during the 16th century. So why not a pint of the best brew here before proceeding to Clee Hill? *C. R. L. Coles*

Titterstone granite is a dark basaltic lava dating back to long before the Ice Age. This hard rock, commercially known as 'Dhu stone' has been quarried from the upper slopes of Clee Hill for many years and there are few roads in the Midlands which have not been metalled with it. This standard gauge mineral railway, part of which was operated by cable haulage, connected the quarry with the main line about half a mile north of Ludlow station. Although this line ceased to operate during 1962, the quarry is still fully operational with an annual output of approximately 200,000 tons.

Clee Hill Mineral Railway

Left:
The upper picture on this page, taken in March 1957, shows Sentinel 0-4-0T No 68164 approaching Clee Hill summit with a train load of 'Dhu stone'.
The lower picture, taken on the same day, shows a loaded wagon train descending the Clee Hill incline having been pushed over the summit by the Sentinel locomotive.
Both: E. J. Dew

Below:
0-4-2ST No 1142 on shunting duty on Clee Hill summit.
Brian Morrison

Bottom:
View looking down from Clee Hill summit towards the Teme valley near Ludlow. The steel cable and supporting rollers are positioned centrally between the two running rails. This and the picture above were taken in August 1958. *Brian Morrison*

Above:
Rebuilt 'Royal Scot' 4-6-0 No 46153 *The Royal Dragoon*
**passing through Ludlow station with a Manchester-
Swansea express in August 1958.** *Brian Morrison*

Below:
Southbound 'Midland Jubilee' headed by 4-6-2 No 6201
Princess Elizabeth **approaching Ludlow in October 1977.**
Brian Morrison

Towards Craven Arms

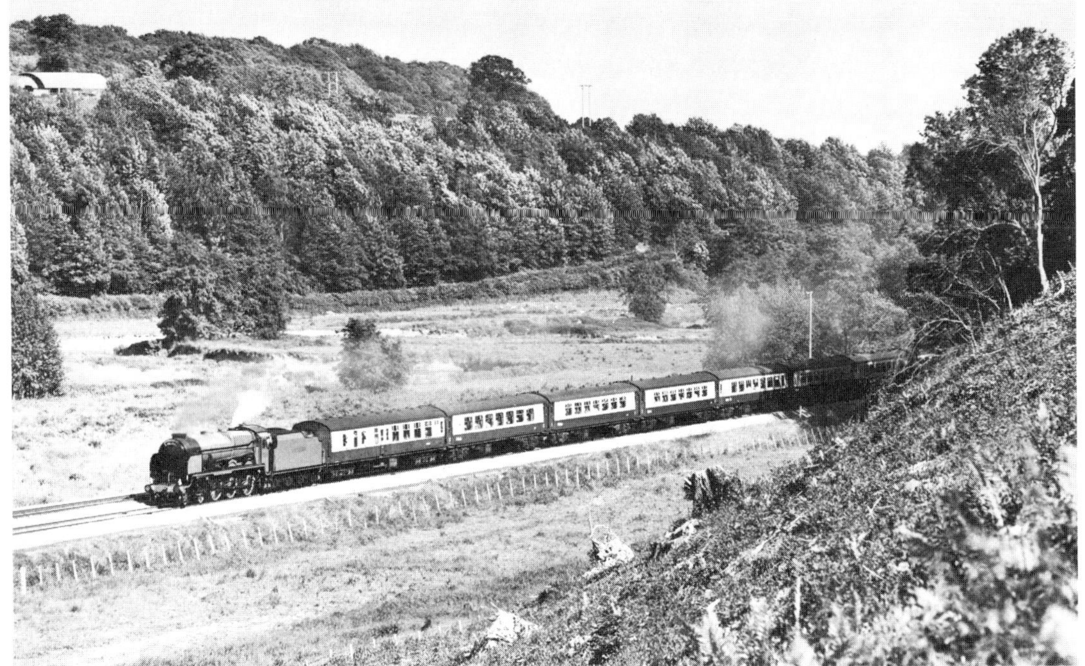

Above:
The Shropshire countryside near Onibury provides a beautiful setting for the 'Cathedrals Pullman', hauled by 4-6-0 No 850 *Lord Nelson*, **as it heads northward on a summer's day in June 1981.** *Peter J. C. Skelton*

Below:
Half a mile further north and the face of the countryside has changed. A few farm buildings amidst the meadows, a Dutch barn (the same barn as in the upper picture) and the River Onny now help to set the scene for 4-6-0 No 5000 as it heads towards Craven Arms with a 'Welsh Marches Pullman' in October 1982. *Dr W. A. Sharman*

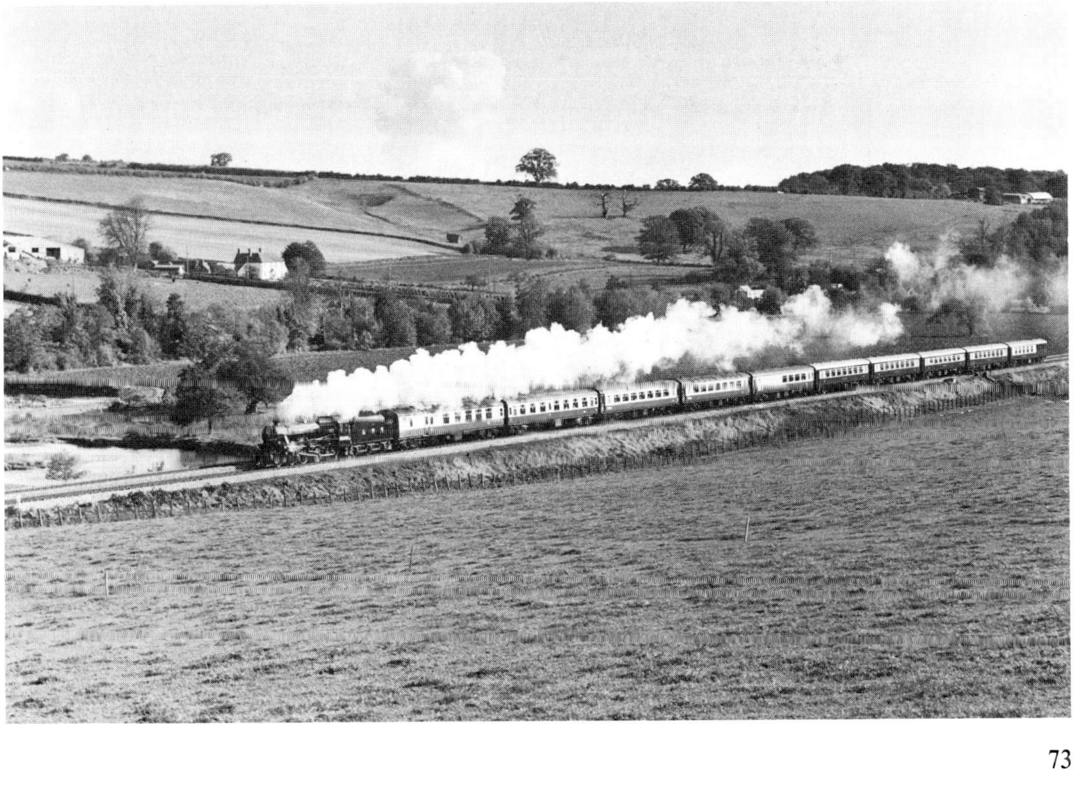

Below:
4-6-0 No 5690 *Leander***, passing Stokesay Castle with a southbound 'Welsh Marches Pullman' in March 1982. The crest of the Long Mynd forms the horizon from left to right whilst on the extreme right, behind the castle is Wenlock Edge.** *Peter J. C. Skelton*

Bottom:
Stokesay Castle as seen from a point adjacent to the railway and with the lake in the foreground. O. S. Nock describes this view as 'one of the choicest scenes on the Welsh border'. *C. R. L. Coles*

Top right:
Hawksworth 4-6-0 No 1003 *County of Wilts* **on a northbound stopping train approaching Craven Arms station in June 1951 (see also P10).** *C. R. L. Coles*

Centre right:
2-8-0 No 2822 approaching Craven Arms station with a southbound goods train in June 1951. *C. R. L. Coles*

Below right:
Fowler 2-6-4T Nos 42305 and 42385 at Craven Arms ready to depart with a train for Swansea (via the Central Wales line) in June 1951. *C. R. L. Coles*

CARLISLE
BISHOPS CASTLE JUNCTION

Bishops Castle Railway

Top left:
Bishops Castle Railway 0-6-0 locomotive *Carlisle* at Craven Arms in May 1932. *H. C. Casserley*

Centre left:
The junction at Stretford Bridge, approximately one mile north of Craven Arms and where the Bishops Castle Railway branched left. *Real Photos*

Bottom left:
0-6-0 locomotive *Carlisle* with a mixed train at Bishops Castle c1930/31. *C. R. L. Coles Collection*

On the Much Wenlock branch

Top:
On the Much Wenlock branch, 2-6-2T No 4409 approaches the station on 10 September 1949 with a two-coach unit from Craven Arms. *H. C. Casserley*

Above:
0-6-0T No 9639 standing in Much Wenlock station with the 7.50am train for Wellington on 21 July 1962.
L. Sandler

Nearing Church Stretton

Above:
Stanier 'Black Five' 4-6-0 No 44835 approaching Marshbrook station in June 1951 with a northbound stopping train for Shrewsbury. *C. R. L. Coles*

Below:
4-6-0 No 5020 *Trematon Castle*, **heading a Cardiff to Manchester express, passing Marshbrook in June 1951.** *C. R. L. Coles*

Above:
Fowler 2-6-4T No 42305 approaching Marshbrook with a train for Swansea (via the Central Wales line) in June 1951. The slopes of the Long Mynd are in the background. *C. R. L. Coles*

Below:
Rebuilt 'Royal Scot' class 4-6-0 No 46160 *Queen Victoria's Rifleman* **approaching Little Stretton with a Plymouth to Manchester express in June 1951.** *C. R. L. Coles*

Storm clouds gather over the Long Mynd as 4-6-0 No 5690 *Leander* heads south near Marshbrook with a 'Welsh Marches Pullman' in March 1982. A considerable area of the Long Mynd range of hills belongs to the National Trust. Comprising approximately 5,500 acres, the property extends for four miles — including the Carding Mill Valley. *Dr W. A. Sharman*

The upper slopes of the Long Mynd set the scene at the trout farm near Marshbrook as the 15.43 train from Shrewsbury to Swansea heads towards Craven Arms on 3 October 1981. *Peter J. C. Skelton*

Above:
Ellsemere Port oil train headed by Class 47 diesel-electric locomotive No 47.076 *City of Truro* **photographed near Marshbrook on 5 June 1982 (See also p59).**
Peter J. C. Skelton

Below:
The summit of Ragleth Hill (1,283ft above sea level) and the woods in the middle distance provide the background scenery as Class 33 No 33.032 heads south near Church Stretton with a Crewe to Cardiff train on 23 October 1982. *Dr W. A. Sharman*

Above:
**Southbound goods train hauled by ex-LNWR 0-8-0
No 49046 passing Ragleth Hill in June 1951. The road at
the foot of the hill, separated from the railway by a field, is
part of Watling Street.** *C. R. L. Coles*

Below:
**Northbound freight train headed by Stanier 2-8-0
No 48492 photographed near Church Stretton in June
1964.** *Derek Cross*

Above:
Welsh ponies provide the story here as, under threatening skies over the Long Mynd, a railtour special heads south near Church Stretton in April 1981. *Dr. W. A. Sharman*

Below:
Bulleid 'Merchant Navy' class 4-6-2 No 35028 *Clan Line* **heading south near Church Stretton on 24 April 1976 with an 'InterCity' special.** *D. Cobbe*

Caer Caradoc provides a scenic background for 4-6-0 No 6000 *King George V* with the Golden Jubilee celebration train, consisting of preserved GWR stock, as it proceeds north from Church Stretton travelling 'wrong road' on 3 July 1977.   *Dr L. A. Nixon*

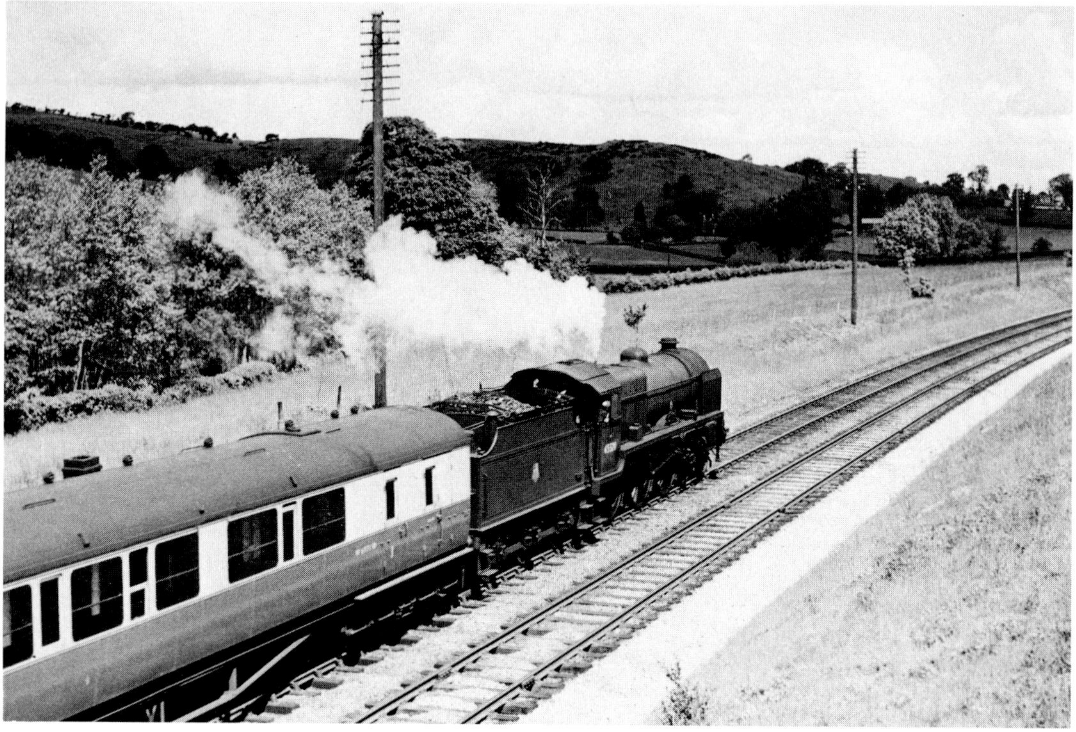

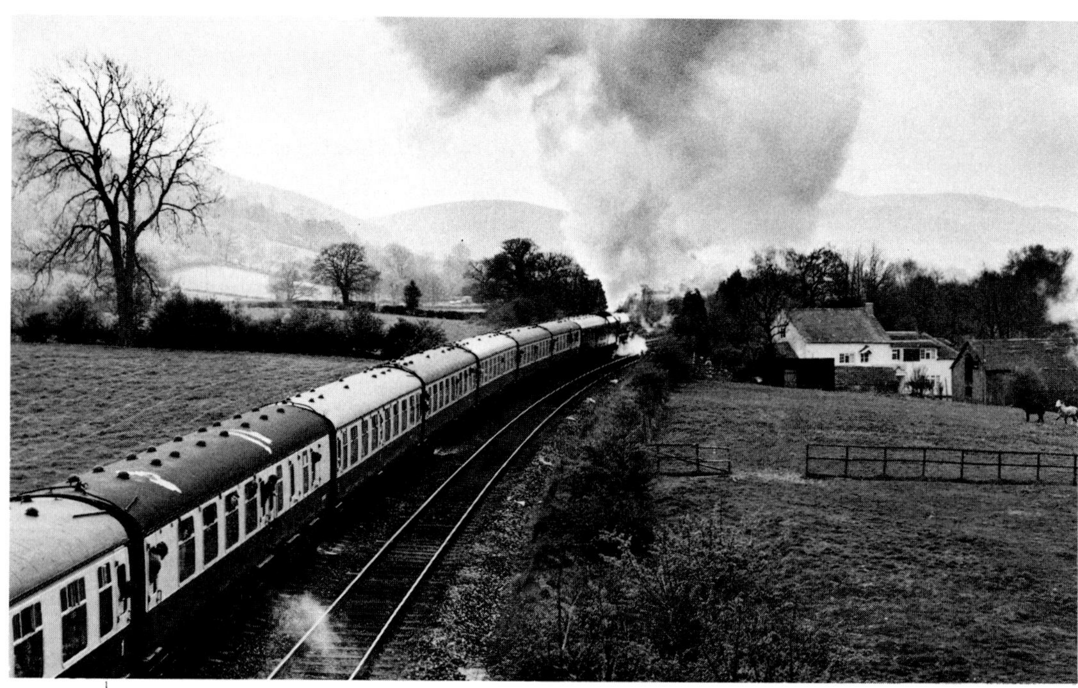

Above:
The 8.55am from Cardiff to Chester and Manchester, hauled by 'Patriot' 4-6-0 No 45520 ***Llandudno*** **coasting downhill between Church Stretton and Leebotwood on 10 June 1957.** *M. Mensing*

Below:
A pictorial rendering of a steam hauled special heading south through the lovely Shropshire countryside near Leebotwood in April 1981. *Peter J. C. Skelton*

Above:
4-6-0s Nos 7812 *Erlestoke Manor* **and 4930** *Hagley Hall* **climbing the 1 in 127 at Bayston Hill, on the outskirts of Shrewsbury, with a 'Welsh Marches Pullman' on 24 April 1982.** *J. S. Whiteley*

Below:
New lightweight diesel railcars forming the 10.49 ex-Shrewsbury for Swansea photographed at the same spot in January 1982. *Dr. W. A. Sharman*

On the Severn Valley Railway

Bridgnorth to Bewdley train, hauled by 4-6-0 No 7819 *Hinton Manor***, crossing the 200ft single span of the Victoria Bridge on 11 August 1978.** *G. D. King*

WD 2-10-0 *Gordon* with a Bridgnorth to Bewdley train photographed on the Victoria Bridge in April 1976.
Brian Morrison

Contrasts at Shrewsbury

Left, Above:
This, and the picture opposite need to be compared with
the title page picture taken at, or near, the same place but
on different occasions during 1981/82. All three are of
4-6-2 No 6201 *Princess Elizabeth* leaving Shrewsbury
with a southbound 'Welsh Marches Pullman'. Yet, because
of the choice of different viewpoints, the three authors
have, unknown to one another, produced widely different
renderings of what is, in effect, the same subject.
Dr W. A. Sharman, J. S. Whiteley

Left:
4-6-0 No 4976 *Warfield Hall* **leaving Shrewsbury with a Hastings to Birkenhead train on 28 August 1952. In the centre road, 2-8-0 No 48706 with a freight train for Crewe awaits the 'right away' whilst on the extreme right (in heavy shadow) is 4-6-0 No 2933** *Bibury Court* **with the then 4.40pm train for Gobowen.** *Brian Morrison*

Below left:
No 2933 *Bibury Court* **gets the green light and makes a brisk departure with the Gobowen train.** *Brian Morrison*

Above:
As Stanier 'Black Five' 4-6-0 No 45037, on a freight for Wrexham, awaits the green light, Hawksworth 4-6-0 No 1025 *County of Radnor* **approaches Shrewsbury in August 1953 with a Chester-Birmingham stopping train.** *Brian Morrison*

Below:
Class 47/3 No 47.318, heading a Llanwern steel train, passing through the station on the same day. The River Severn flows beneath the nearer platform ramps — one of the bridge parapets being on the extreme right of the picture. *Brian Morrison*

Left:
'Star' class 4-6-0 No 4049 *Princess Maud* **had just arrived with an express from Paddington, which it had worked from Wolverhampton, when this picture was taken in August 1952.** *Brian Morrison*

Below:
Acquired by the Shropshire & Montgomeryshire Railway in 1910, 0-6-0ST *Morous* **was later found to lack the necessary power to enable it to give satisfactory service on that line. Accordingly in 1924, Colonel Stephens, at that time the General Manager of the S&MR, had it transferred to another light railway which was also under his management — the West Sussex Railway where it remained in service until the latter closed down in January 1935. This could well be one of the last pictures to be taken of** *Morous*, **here seen in the galvanised iron shed at Selsey in December of that year and still showing evidence of previous ownership on the saddle tank.** *Morous* **was scrapped on site during the following year.** *C. R. L. Coles*

Right:
Class 101 DMU cars M51201/56347 forming the
12.40pm train for Crewe photographed outside
Shrewsbury station on 14 September 1981. The column in
the background, which is 133ft 6in high, and is the highest
Greek Doric column in the world, was erected in 1814/16
in memory of Lord Rowland Hill, Shrewsbury's most
distinguished soldier and the Duke of Wellington's right
hand man both in the Peninsular wars and at the Battle of
Waterloo. *Brian Morrison*

Below:
Metro-Cammell Class 101 DMU No M51200 heading the
10.17 train from Aberystwyth approaching Shrewsbury on
14 September 1981. The Abbey church dominating this
picture dates back to 1083 and is all that remains of a
Benedictine foundation dedicated to SS Peter and Paul.
The Great West tower was built in the 14th century during
the reign of Edward III. The Great West window (to the
right of the clockface) is of Heraldic glass and dates from
the reign of Richard II. *Brian Morrison*

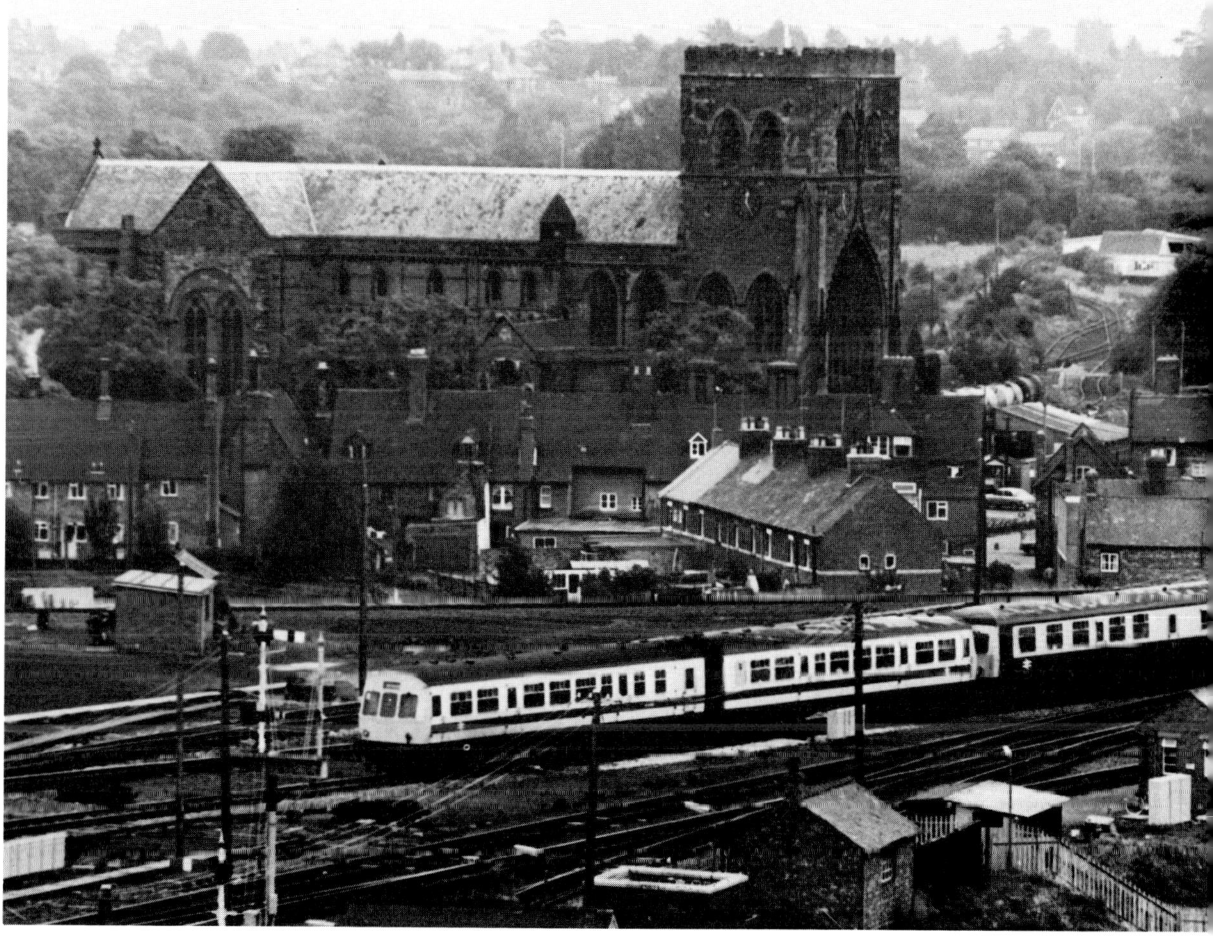

Left:
Shrewsbury has to its credit more than 1,000 buildings, of which the railway station is one, which are listed for protection by the Department of the Environment.

Designed by T. Penson, Junior, the building is of Grinshill (Shropshire) stone in the Gothic style, the recessed centre having a grid of horizontal Tudor windows with diamond glazing, and a symmetrically placed embattled tower. The actual construction of the station was carried out by Thomas Brassey and it was opened on 12 October 1848 to serve the then Shrewsbury & Chester Railway. *Graham Vincent*

Centre left:
Belvidere Bridge which carries the main line from Birmingham across the River Severn on the outskirts of Shrewsbury was cast at Coalbrookdale in 1848 — some 13 years earlier than the Victoria Bridge at Arley (Severn Valley Railway p88). Designed by William Baker, this twin-arched structure is in course of being strengthened and modernised. Except that the old cast ornamental balustrades will be replaced by box tubing safety rails, the overall appearance of this bridge will remain generally unaltered. *L. Davies*

Below:
Shrewsbury Castle, adjacent to the railway station, was originally built during Norman times. The oldest surviving parts of the present building date from the reign of Henry II. It was refurbished as a residence in 1790 by Thomas Telford and, in 1924, presented to the town by the Shropshire Horticultural Society. It is now used as a museum. *Shrewsbury Information Centre*

Below:
The River Severn describes a horse-shoe bend round the centre of Shrewsbury and 10 bridges cross the river giving access to the town itself. The English Bridge, shown in this picture, is the second to be built at this point, to the designs of John Gwynn, and opened in 1774. In 1925 the bridge was dismantled stone by stone and reconstructed two years later using local Grinshill stone. It measures 50ft between the parapets compared with 23ft 6in of the earlier bridge. *Shrewsbury Information Centre*

Below left:
The Abbot's House in Butcher Row is one of many half-timbered buildings in Shrewsbury and dates back to c1450. Butcher Row is one of several medieval streets which, back in the 11th century, were named after the traders who either lived or carried out their business in them.
Shrewsbury Information Centre

Below right:
Rowley's House, a particularly fine example of a 16th century timber-framed house, contains the greatest single collection of relics excavated from the nearby Roman city of Viriconium. Part of this house is supported by stout wooden timbers — as shown in this picture. The buses in the adjoining bus station — could they be serving some of the rural places which once enjoyed the sight of an ex-GWR pannier tank engine with its two carriages?
C. R. L. Coles

Shrewsbury to Chester

The concluding $42\frac{1}{2}$ miles to Chester are over a series of reverse gradients, the steepest of which extends for nearly four miles at 1 in 83, favouring down trains, near Gresford. It was here that, in 1934, the worst mining disaster within living memory took place when more than 200 lives were lost in an underground explosion. The pit in question was subsequently sealed off and remains so to this day.

No less than eight branch lines diverged from this route in various directions; the longest of these was from Ruabon to Barmouth. Whittington (now closed), Gobowen and Wrexham were the other three interchange stations for the connecting branch trains. All of these branches have either been closed completely or are now only open for goods traffic — in the Gobowen/Oswestry and Wrexham districts and even here, only parts remain in use. Of the Ruabon-Barmouth branch a short stretch of line has been preserved at Llangollen (including the station) and is now under the care of the Llangollen Railway Society. The station here, adjacent to the River Dee, is a very pretty former GWR station and is close to the 600-year old stone bridge spanning both river and railway. Known as the 'Bridge of Friendship', this bridge brings back many happy memories of 1977 when, in glorious summer sunshine, I spent two days at Llangollen photographing some of the many visitors from overseas who had gathered here to take part in the International Musical Eisteddfod. This annual event is held during the first full week in July when the competitors, dressed in their colourful national costumes, mingle in the festival arena and in the town itself in ever changing scenes. No introductions and no interpreters are needed — the language of music and friendship being international. Some of these visitors were even taking advantage of steam train rides organised by the Llangollen Railway Society during the week of the Eisteddfod.

But now it is back to Gobowen, one of the terminal points of the former Cambrian Railways and, before closure for passenger traffic, one of the two junctions for Oswestry and a number of small remote places in former Montgomeryshire. Between here and Ruabon are the two principal civil engineering features of this line — the viaducts at Chirk and Cefn Mawr. The former, alongside which is an aqueduct at a lower level, carries the railway over the River Ceiriog. The aqueduct carries the Shropshire Union Canal which passes beneath the railway near this point. The viaduct at Cefn Mawr is, like that at Chirk, no less imposing. It carries the railway across the Vale of Llangollen through which flows the River Dee. Mention of Chirk recalls the Glyn Valley Tramway which was built to the unusual gauge of 2ft $4\frac{1}{2}$in and opened in March 1874. It ran up the Ceiriog Valley for a distance of nine miles and, for many years, earned its revenue by the movement of heavy slates to the main line at Chirk. The opening of a granite quarry at Hendre in 1875 led to increased traffic until, in more recent years, this succumbed to road transport. The introduction of road motor buses in 1932 also contributed to its final demise — the tramway finally closing in 1935.

Wrexham, to which reference has already been made, is now known as Wrexham General — this to distinguish it from two other stations in the town, Exchange and Central. Both these latter are served by what was formerly an outpost of the former Great Central Railway over which British Rail operates a local service between Wrexham Central and Birkenhead.

The approach to Chester is from a westerly direction — the railway over the final two miles using the same tracks as the main Chester-Holyhead line. We have now reached the end of our tour, in good time for dinner and an overnight stop. Much could be written about the City of Chester — the ancient Roman fortress of Deva which dates back to the middle of the 1st century AD. The red sandstone walls were built by the Romans early in the 2nd century and rebuilt in AD907 by Ethelfreda, Lady of the Mercians, since when their line has remained unchanged.

Tomorrow it will be Sunday so what could be better than a brisk walk round these walls after breakfast before morning service in the cathedral the history of which can also be traced back to AD907. Also built of red sandstone, this hallowed building, as we know it today, dates back to 1092 and was originally a Benedictine abbey until the dissolution of the monasteries after which, in 1541, it became the cathedral of the newly formed diocese of Chester.

After lunch it is, once more, back to the railway station (where routes converge from no less than six different directions) but, this time, for our journey home.

Above:
The 'Black Countryman', yet another steam-hauled special, with 4-6-0 No 5000 piloting standard 2-6-4T No 80079, passing Coton Hill yard in April 1980 en route for Chester and Manchester (Victoria). *Dr L. A. Nixon*

Below:
'A4' class 4-6-2 No 4498 *Sir Nigel Gresley* **approaching Shrewsbury with the Chester-Salop portion of the 'Midland Jubilee' on 1 October 1977.** *Brian Morrison*

Left:
Two of the locomotives preserved by the Severn Valley Railway — Ivatt 2-6-0 No 43106 and 4-6-0 No 7812 *Erlestoke Manor* — passing Leaton with a 'Welsh Marches Pullman' on 5 June 1982 prior to a water stop at Baschurch. *Peter J. C. Skelton*

Bottom:
This four-wheeled divisional engineers' saloon was one of a number which were converted from ex-Bristol & Exeter vehicles originally built in 1875 as six-wheeled composites. They had verandahs at each end and were equipped with Victorian style interior furnishings. This particular example may well have been the Wolverhampton saloon and the last to survive. Its number unknown, it had been parked in a siding at Warwick for many months during 1950 by which time it was at least 80 years old, (See also p102). *Ian Allan Library*

The Spirit of Llangollen

Top right:
Ruabon station: Change here for Llangollen, Corwen, Ruthin, Bala, Festiniog, Dolgelley and Barmouth. A 1949 picture. *Real Photographs (19276)*

Centre right:
Although the branch from Ruabon no longer exists, the railway station at Llangollen has, happily, been preserved by the Llangollen Railway Society. This picture with the River Dee in the foreground, was taken in August 1960 showing a train from Bala hauled by 0-6-0PT No 7442. This station was regarded as being one of the prettiest on the former Great Western Railway. During the week of the International Musical Eisteddfod, the Llangollen Railway Society organise steam train rides for the benefit of the many hundreds of visitors and competitors converging on this beautiful part of the Border country. *Derek Cross*

EISTEDDFOD
LLANGOLLEN
CORWEN RUABON
BALA FESTINIOG

Bottom:
Wherever you may be, the spirit of friendship is ever
present during the week of the Eisteddfod. This picture of a
group of Macedonian instrumentalists giving an
impromptu performance by the River Dee (and within
sight of the railway station) evokes that spirit.
C. R. L. Coles

Left:
Once the junction for Oswestry and beyond, Gobowen station looking north in April 1955. *Real Photos (K2511)*

Below:
0-4-2T No 1164 with four-wheeled inspection coach standing in Oswestry station in 1936. Note the express passenger headcode. The station building here was, at one time, the administrative headquarters of the former Cambrian Railways. In later years this was transferred to Shrewsbury. *C. R. L. Coles*

Bottom:
'Duke' class 4-4-0 Nos 3291 *Severn* and 3290 *Thames* at Oswestry in 1936 on a train for Welshpool and mid-Wales. *C. R. L. Coles*

Below:

Chirk Viaduct, which carries the railway across the valley through which flows the River Ceiriog, photographed on 26 February 1967. Crossing the viaduct is the LCGB 'Severn and Dee' railtour en route from Wolverhampton LL to Chester and hauled by 4-6-0 No 7029 *Clun Castle.* **Seen through the arches on the left of the picture is the aqueduct which carries the Shropshire Union Canal across this valley.** *Brian Stephenson*

Bottom:

Preserved Collett 0-6-2T No 6697, heading a SLS special from Wolverhampton to Chester, photographed on 27 March 1966 when crossing Chirk viaduct. The Shropshire Union Canal is to the left of the picture.
Brian Stephenson

Below:
On the Glyn Valley Tramway. A scene at Glynceiriog in August 1926. The locomotive is named *Sir Theodore.*
H. C. Casserley

Bottom:
The viaduct at Cefn Mawr spans the valley through which flows the River Dee. In this picture an inter-city enthusiast's special is seen crossing the viaduct in September 1979 on its journey from Chester to Hereford. It has 19 arches each with a span of 60ft, a total length of 1,508ft and is 147ft high. *Peter J. C. Skelton*

Right:
No 7029 *Clun Castle* **coasting down Gresford bank past the site of Gresford station with the 'Severn and Dee' railtour on 26 February 1967.** *Brian Stephenson*

Below right:
'A4' class 4-6-2 No 4498 *Sir Nigel Gresley* **had plenty of steam to spare when climbing Gresford bank (1 in 82) with 'The Salopian' on 16 May 1981.** *Dr W. A. Sharman*

Chester — From Many Angles

Below:
A very strong pictorial impression of 4-6-2 No 46229 *Duchess of Hamilton* rounding the curve near Saltney Junction, Chester, with a 'Welsh Marches Pullman' in October 1982. *Dr L. A. Nixon*

Bottom:
Heading the 'Deeside Venturer' 4-6-0 No 6000 *King George V* is here seen crossing the bridge over the River Dee at Chester in October 1980 en route for Shrewsbury.

Until comparatively recently this bridge carried an additional two tracks forming the main line from Chester to Holyhead. All traffic is now concentrated on the former GWR metals. Chester racecourse is to the right of the picture. *Peter J. C. Skelton*

Right:
Class 40 No 40.047 with a westbound ballast train passing Chester No 4 signalbox in September 1981.
Brian Morrison

Below right:
Chester No 6 signalbox. *Dr L. A. Nixon*

Left:
Class 40 No 40.155 leaving Chester with a Manchester-Holyhead Freightliner in April 1979. *J. S. Whiteley*

Below:
The Shropshire Union Grand Canal (or part of it) which closely follows the city wall from Northgate lock to Cow Lane Bridge and Christleton is a popular tourist attraction in Chester — visitors being taken through the locks by horse-drawn barges. In this picture an express for Llandudno is seen crossing the canal at Northgate lock in July 1978. *D. A. Flitcroft*

Right:
Class 47/3 No 47.447 heading the 13.00 Euston to Holyhead express photographed from the city walls in Chester at the point where the railway crosses the Shropshire Union Canal at Northgate lock. This picture was taken in August 1977. *Dr. L. A. Nixon*

Above:
Class 40 No 40.076 passing Chester No 2 signalbox at the east end of Chester station with an express from Llandudno to York on 19 September 1981.
Brian Morrison

Below:
'Black Five' 4-6-0 No 5305 photographed on 18 April 1981 at the same spot with a railtour excursion returning to Hull. *J. S. Whiteley*

Above:
'5XP' 4-6-0 No 5710 *Irresistible* **and an unidentified ex-LNWR 'George V' class 4-4-0 at Chester station in 1937.** *C. R. L. Coles*

Below:
Signal gantry (since dismantled) adjacent to Chester No 4 signalbox photographed in July 1966. *Dr L. A. Nixon*

Above:
The city walls round Chester extend over a distance of approximately two miles. This picture shows the walls and the Newgate. Displaying the arms of the city, the Prince of Wales (Earl of Chester) and of the Grosvenor, Stanley and Egerton families, none of which is visible in this picture, this gate was built in 1938 — replacing an older gate which was too narrow for present-day traffic. In the foreground is the Roman garden containing Roman remains found in the city, including a hypocaust.
Chester City Council

Below left:
Eastgate. The clock on the footbridge commemorates Queen Victoria's diamond jubilee.
Vernon D. Shaw/Chester City Council

Below right:
Chester Cathedral from the southwest — as seen from the Cheshire Regiment memorial garden.   *C. R. L. Coles*

WELSH
MARCHES
PULLMAN
Z42